Neville Richardson

The World Council of Churches and
Race Relations: 1960 to 1969

Studien zur interkulturellen Geschichte des Christentums
Études d'Histoire Interculturelle du Christianisme
Studies in the Intercultural History of Christianity

Herausgegeben von/edité par/edited by

| Richard Friedli | Walter J. Hollenweger | Hans Jochen Margull |
| Université de Fribourg | University of Birmingham | Universität Hamburg |

Band 9

Neville Richardson

The World Council of Churches and
Race Relations: 1960 to 1969

Peter Lang Frankfurt/M.
Herbert Lang Bern
1977

Neville Richardson

The World Council of Churches and Race Relations: 1960 to 1969

Peter Lang Frankfurt/M.
Herbert Lang Bern
1977

ISBN 3 261 01718 X

©

Peter Lang GmbH, Frankfurt/M. (BRD)
Herbert Lang & Cie AG, Bern (Schweiz)
1977. alle Rechte vorbehalten

Nachdruck oder Vervielfältigung, auch auszugsweise, in allen Formen wie Mikrofilm, Xerographie, Mikrofiche, Mikrocard, Offset verboten.

Druck: fotokop wilhelm weihert KG, Darmstadt

CONTENTS

		Page
INTRODUCTION		7
CHAPTER I:	The Matrix of World Council Thought on Race Relations	11
CHAPTER II:	Policy and Action - I: Contact, Consultation and Statement	19
CHAPTER III:	New Directions in the Social Thought of the World Council of Churches	35
CHAPTER IV:	Policy and Action - II: Confrontation and Conflict	49
CONCLUSION		61
APPENDIX		65
NOTES		67
BIBLIOGRAPHY		75

INTRODUCTION

The World Council of Churches is the chief manifestation in the world today of the ecumenical movement. It would be a mistake, however, to identify the Council with the movement. Many instances of ecumenism are to be found outside the World Council of Churches. Stirrings have been felt in the Roman Catholic Church which led to the establishment of the Secretariat for Christian Unity in the Vatican in 1958. Ecumenism has also long been among the main motivating forces in the Young Men's Christian Associations and the Student Christian Movements.

The word ecumenical (oecumenical) is defined in the Oxford Dictionary as:

> 1. <u>Eccl.</u> Belonging to or representing the whole (Christian) world, or the universal church; general, universal, catholic; <u>spec.</u> applied to the general councils of the early church, and (in mod. use) of the Roman Catholic Church ...
> 2. <u>gen.</u> Belonging to the whole world; universal, general, worldwide.

The word has various meanings, but its present, most typical one is that which was adopted by the Oxford Conference in 1937.

> The term ecumenical refers to the expression within history of the given unity of the Church. The thought and action of the Church are ecumenical, in so far as they attempt to realize the Una Sancta, the followship of Christians, who acknowledge the one Lord.

This is the sense in which the word will be used.

As the title suggests, attention, is focussed on the World Council of Churches as the chief among many manifestations of the ecumenical movement. Therefore we shall not attempt to deal with the considerable interest and activity of other ecumenical bodies, such as those referred to above, or of the various national and regional councils of churches, in the matter of race relations.

Reference will be made periodically to "the thought" or "the thinking" of the World Council. It must be pointed out that this is a problematic concept. Its use involves an unavoidable measure of generalization. The difficulty stems from the nature of the World Council and its relationship with its constituent churches. In its constitution it is defined as follows:

> The World Council of Churches is a fellowship of churches which confess the Lord Jesus Christ as God and Saviour according to the Scriptures and therefore seek to fulfil together their common calling to the glory of the one God, Father, Son and Holy Spirit.(1)

This "fellowship" is by no means a homogeneous whole and agreement on matters of thought and action is not always unanimous. The decisions which are embodied in statements and resolutions, while supported by the majority, are not necessarily the view of all the nember churches, nor are they in any way binding on the churches. The constitution makes clear both the nature of the authority of the statements and the limits imposed upon that authority by the autonomy of the member churches.

> While such statements may have great significance and influence as the expression of the judgement or concern of so widely representative a Christian body, yet their authority will consist only in the weight which they carry by their own truth and wisdom and the publishing of such statements shall not be held to imply that the World Council as such has, or can have, any constitutional authority over the constituent churches or right to speak for them. (2)

Even more problematic is the concept of race. Liston Pope points out that, as far as scientific knowledge is concerned, "race" is an almost meaningless term. He suggests "common stock" as a preferable alternative. (3) Visser't Hooft, likewise, admits his difficulty in using the term. (4) He sees "the race problem" as being not so much a biological as a sociological problem in which theological, cultural and psychological factors all play their part. This difficulty is compounded by the fact that in some cases the problem springs from ethnic rather than racial factors. What Visser't Hooft means by the two terms is not altogether clear. He does not attempt to define them but simply states, correctly in our view, that it would be artificial to draw a hard and fast line between the two. In this thesis "ethnicity" is taken to be the wider concept of the two and, as such, includes cultural, religious and racial factors. "Race" is understood as usually involving characteristics among which colour is dominant.

For this reason we shall not deal with the Christian approach to Jews, although this topic has exercised ecumenical thinking almost throughout this century. At the 1937 Oxford Conference the "Jewish question" did become, with the impact of Nazi mythology, a racial question and was treated as such by the churches. During our period, however, the characteristics which distinguish Jewish people are seen to pertain to culture and religion rather than to colour and race.

Problematic though it may be, the term "race" is indispensable. It refers to a reality in the world which cannot be ignored. It is a powerful component in economic, political and social relationships, but it most certainly cannot be reduced without remainder to economic, political or social categories.

Given the nature of the ecumenical movement in general and of the World Council of Churches in particular, it is no surprise that race relations has become a central concern. The universal perspective and the drive towards unity are, in essence, at odds with all those forces which make for division within the Christian family and within the family of mankind. As Visser't Hooft points out:

> ... the race problem is so obviously a world problem and the
> repercussions of inter-racial conflict in one area on the racial
> situation in other areas are so considerable, that these issues
> become inevitably a central subject of ecumenical concern between
> the Churches.(5)

The popular image of the church as regards race relations is also vital to its missionary enterprise. Kitagawa is fearful that this image has been badly tarnished. He cites Africa as a case in which growing scepticism about the moral integrity of the Christian church has been driving the "intellectuals" towards Marxism and the masses towards Islam. For the African, Christianity is the religion of the white man. Kitagawa detects, at the root of the problem, a lack of trust between Christians of different races. This is a problem of critical proportions for the church.

> Not to trust other Christians and not to be trusted by them is for
> a Christian little short of receiving a death sentence. If the church
> has in any way and to any degree been responsible for the Negro
> Christian's lack of confidence in the white Christians or in the
> leadership of the church in general, the church must immediately
> do everything in her power to regain the Negro Christian's confidence.
> Otherwise the church is bound to lose her own soul, however successful and prosperous she may be in every other way.(6)

In addition to the terms "ecumenical" and "race", three others need to be clarified. Western refers to the established, mostly wealthy and predominantly white regions and nations around the North Atlantic, namely Western Europe and North America. It also includes those groups of people in other parts of the world who are of Western European origin and whose language and culture are basically European. The dominant religion of "the West" is Christianity. The third world is comprised of countries distinct from those of "the West" in that they are new to international economic and political relationships. Included in this category are countries in Africa, Central and South America, and Asia. Many of them have only recently received independent status. Generally they are far poorer than the "Western" nations and their people and culture are not of European origin. Christianity, which is seldom the traditional religion, takes its place as one faith among many in these countries. The younger churches are those which were established, mainly in the "third world", by the missionary thrust of the nineteenth and early twentieth centuries. Originally they came under the direction of the Western missionary bodies but, especially since the Second World War, most of them have become autonomous. It should be pointed out that these terms are by no means precise, but are useful generalizations.

As the title suggests, this thesis is both historical and evaluative. This has presented a practical difficulty. It will be noticed that sometimes the past tense is used and sometimes the present. In describing the events which have occurred the past tense is employed, but in discussing the nature and value of the thought and action it has seemed natural to use the present.

Finally, abbreviations are used as sparingly as possible. For the sake of convenience, however, in the notes and at their second and subsequent mention in each chapter, a few lengthy titles are abbreviated as follows:

I.M.C.	The International Missionary Council
P.C.R.	The Programme to Combat Racism
The Secretariat	The Secretariat for Racial and Ethnic Relations
The World Council or W.C.C.	The World Council of Churches.

Assemblies and major consultations are frequently referred to by the name of the venue, thus:

Amsterdam	The First Assembly of the World Council of Churches, 1948.
Evanston	The Second Assembly of the World Council of Churches, 1954.
New Delhi	The Third Assembly of the World Council of Churches, 1961.
Uppsala	The Fourth Assembly of the World Council of Churches, 1968.
Cottesloe	The Consultation on the churches and race relations in South Africa, held in Johannesburg, 1960.
Mindolo	The Ecumenical Consultation on Christian Practice and Desirable Action in Social Change and Race Relations in Southern Africa held in Kitwe, Zambia, 1964.
Notting Hill	The World Council of Churches Sponsored Consultation on Racism held in London, 1969.

Chapter I
THE MATRIX OF WORLD COUNCIL THOUGHT ON RACE RELATIONS

In 1960 the Secretariat for Racial and Ethnic Relations was new to the structure of the World Council. The initiatives from which it sprang were by no means new. It owed its origin to a resolution of the Second Assembly held in Evanston, U.S.A., in 1954. It owed its nature and methods in the main to the patterns of ethical thought which were operative at Evanston.

At the inaugural Assembly in Amsterdam in 1948, the serious nature of race problems had been recognized. Because of its other priorities, however, the Assembly could not afford those problems the attention they deserved. The first priority was the convergence of the main streams of the ecumenical movement and the provision of a new basis for fellowship between the various Christian denominations, despite wide differences in tradition and theology. Race problems were viewed in this context. They were forces which made for division and were thrown into sharp relief by the general sense of a growing unity. The Message of the Assembly sees pride of nation, race and class as a threat to ecumenical unity and churches are urged on the local level to oppose race discrimination. Such discrimination is especially condemned where it exists within the life of certain churches. In the Section on "The Universal Church in God's Design", it is confessed with shame that the evils of the world have permeated into the churches so that the divisions between churches are not only theological. The non-theological factors are especially dangerous.

> Even where there are no differences of theology, language or liturgy, there exist churches segregated by race and colour, a scandal within the Body of Christ. We are in danger of being salt that has lost its savour and is fit for nothing. (7)

In Section III on "The Church and the Disorder of Society" the church is seen to have a clear mandate from God to call society away from prejudice based on race and colour and from the practices of discrimination and segregation which are denials of justice and human dignity. The primary practical step to be taken by the church is that of improving the quality of its own life.

> ... it cannot say a convincing word to society unless it takes steps to eliminate these practices from the Christian community, because they contradict all that it believes about God's love for all His children. (8)

This step as a prerequisite to further action is both valid and obvious. The interesting point is the seeming inability or unwillingness of the Assembly to say anything further. The kind of action to be pursued and the specific areas in which it would be appropriate are not mentioned. Clearly the Assembly was keen to avoid anything which might jeopardize the coming together and staying together of the churches. For example, a suggestion was made at a meeting of Section III to condemn segregation in principle and to deplore explicitly the toleration of the system in South African and American churches. The suggestion was rejected.

It was in 1950 that a specific case was demarcated for consideration. The Central Committee, meeting in Toronto, adopted a proposal that a multi-racial delegation be sent to South Africa under the auspices of the World Council and the International Missionary Council, should the churches in that country be willing to issue an invitation. The stated objective was "conference and fellowship". In their replies the member churches and the Christian Council of South Africa were in general agreement that the time was not opportune for such a visit. Instead, they issued an invitation to the General Secretary. It was accepted and, in 1952, Dr. W. A. Visser 't Hooft visited South Africa. His observations and recommendations on the complexities of the racial problem and the conflicting policies of church groups were presented to the Central Committee at Lucknow in 1953. (9) The main thrust of his suggestions is that there should be more study on the subject of race, especially on the relevant biblical teaching, and that contact should be increased between the South African churches and those in other parts of the world. The response of the Central Committee was to pass a resolution, incorporating a quotation from the Amsterdam Report, condemning racial discrimination.

A number of people were unhappy that race relations had not been treated as a subject in its own right by the Amsterdam Assembly. Sir Kenneth Grubb, chairman of the Commission of the Churches on International Affairs, had urged strongly that it be included as a major subject on the agenda, but to no avail. Grubb writes:

> I well remember, at a committee on the Continent shortly after the war, arguing that racialism was bound soon to become one of the grim "running sores" of the world; and for the Christian Church where was "neither Jew nor Greek, bond nor free" this was a serious challenge. I begged that it should be a major subject at the First Assembly of the World Council of Churches in Amsterdam in 1948. Dr. Visser 't Hooft, the General secretary, agreed, but others did not. The subject was certainly mentioned, but it was not until the Evanston Assembly in 1954 that a special section was set up to study it and issue a statement. (10)

The <u>Second Assembly</u> did indeed provide the opportunity for a full discussion on race relations. One of its Sections was entitled, "Intergroup Relations: The Church Amid Racial and Ethnic Tensions." Not so much a significant advance, Evanston was rather a crystallizing of ecumenical thought on the subject thus far. In this respect it is a milestone.

The impression is conveyed in the preparatory material that the intention was to provide a base for practical solutions to the problem. The organizers seem to have felt that enough had been said on the fact of racial prejudice and on the attitude of the churches. There is a hint of impatience in the request that appropriate methods be established to guide the churches in their actions. The general question to be answered was: "How can the Church contribute to the correction of racial prejudice and injustice?" It was specified that what was required was neither a definite Christian position on race, nor a sociological analysis. Both of these would be involved, however, in the answering of the crucial practical question: "What can concretely be done?" Three main areas were to be dealt with under this general head.

1. How can the message of the Gospel be presented so as to affect the deep springs of race prejudice?
2. How should the Christian Church deal with race within its own membership (in order to exemplify Christian conviction on the matter)?
3. How may the Christian community utilize and co-operate with government and other secular agencies in the alleviation of racial injustice?(11)

These suggestions were too optimistic. They assumed that answers to the questions were freely available on the basis of previous social thought. They did not anticipate the immensity of the scope of the empirical analyses of particular situations that was required.

Despite the good intentions of Evanston and its obvious contribution in drawing together the strands of ecumenical thinking on race relations, Evanston cannot be said to be a significant advance in that thinking. It was essentially the same in its approach, for instance, as J.H. Oldham who published his <u>Christianity and the Race Problem</u> in 1924. This was the first thorough attempt at a sustained treatment of race in its relation to the Christian faith. It sprang out of Oldham's special concern, as secretary of the I.M.C., for Africa south of the Sahara.

Oldham made no attempt to elaborate a set of rules for Christians to follow. He was of the opinion that it was not the purpose of a Christian ethic to give explicit rules in regard to such specific problems as race. The New Testament cannot supply us with a detailed social programme and we should not try to create such a programme as part of our doctrine. Oldham's fundamental view of Christianity is that it is:

> ... first and foremost not a code of morality but a religion ... not primarily a command but a Gospel.(12)

As such it makes a distinctive contribution to man's moral life. By its appeal to man's whole personality rather than to his intellect alone, Christianity supplies him with:

> ... an outlook, a temper, a spirit which more than anything else is capable of bringing harmony into the relations of men with one another.(13)

At Evanston there were those, particularly in the Reformed tradition, who saw ethics and doctrine as an inseparable unity which must be derived from the Bible. There were also those who felt that the correct approach to race relations was the formulation of a set of rules deduced from general principles. Ir its pronouncements, however, Evanston is substantially in agreement with the method of Oldham. Its concern is to influence attitudes and not to issue a code of conduct.

In his concept of man, Oldham tries to strike a balance between the corporate and the individual aspects. On the one hand the

> ... true life of a man is that of a person in relation with other persons.

On the other while we must, for instance, acknowledge the significance of race,

> ... we must not ... allow it to obscure from us the reality, uniqueness and value of the individual. (14)

Oldham acknowledges the validity of the general argument of the social gospel which so strongly influenced the first Life and Work Conference, held in Stockholm in 1925. He is aware that race prejudice is not only a matter of individual attitudes but that it is fostered by the institutions of society. Racial problems are seen largely as social, political and economic problems. So long as the world's wealth remains unequally divided and power remains unequally shared, racial rivalry and conflict will threaten. The British Empire, therefore, should operate strictly on the basis of trusteeship and any benefits of trade and development should benefit equally the countries concerned. The objective should be the creation of a social and international situation in which human relationships are enriched rather than hindered by racial differences. There can be no doubt, however, that although he makes these observations, Oldham sees the relationship of individual with individual as primary and that of group with group as secondary. The social and corporate are, in the end, reducible to individual units.

> The basis of society is individual character, and the ultimate social and political problem is the building of character. (15)

Evanston, likewise, is aware of the institutional aspects of racial prejudice, but the method it uses reveals an underlying individualism. The assumption was that if a man was provided with the necessary information and given opportunities for personal contact with people of different races, his attitudes would be transformed and healthy race relations would follow. It was hoped that official statements of the World Council, together with the fellow ship of the ecumenical movement would fulfil these requirements.

In at least three respects Evanston differed from Oldham's thinking. First, it spoke, as Oldham could not at the time of writing his book, from within the World Council of Churches. Evanston spoke conscious of the fact that what it said was the voice of non-Roman Christendom. Its statements carried authority and were regarded confidently as the most important means by which men's attitudes would be changed and a solution brought to the race problems of the world. Also, the primary locus of activity is the new international fellow ship of the churches and the subsequently strengthened life of the local congregation. Only indirectly, through the witness and challenge of the churches, is society to be changed. The hope which the newly-fledged World Council generated is characterized in the thought of W.A. Visser 't Hooft. His <u>The Ecumenical Movement and the Racial Problem</u>, written just before the Evanston Assembly, agrees with Oldham and with the Oxford

Conference of 1937 in most major areas. Racial differences, for instance, are accepted as positive and enriching aspects of human life, and it is fully recognized that race prejudice becomes embedded in and perpetuated by social institutions. The growing ecumenical fellowship, however, is seen as the new and most hopeful centre from which to tackle the problem. Individual attitudes must be changed and this cannot be done by normal means of education. This is because of the nature of racial prejudice.

> ... racial prejudice is not just a form of ignorance which can be progressivly dispelled by enlightenment or by the proclamation of the ideal of racial understanding. Pride can only be overcome by a force which makes for humility. An ego-centric will-to-power can only be counteracted by a deep sense of responsibility for those who are in danger of becoming the victims of that attitude. (16)

Obsessional fear is dispelled only by the security which is the gift of faith in God's sovereign rule. The task of the World Council, then, is to assist the churches in their efforts to bring about changed attitudes by impressing their distinctive Christian contribution to the situation. Churches must be helped to maintain a constant tension between their fundamental Christian convictions and social realities, but also to observe their pastoral responsibility to their members not to "go too far ahead" of them and thus lose contact and with it the opportunity for influence. The hope was that by pursuing this method the churches, inspired and encouraged by the ecumenical movement, would bring about a change of attitude in enough individuals to change public opinion at large.

The second point of difference from Oldham's thought was the eschatological emphasis at Evanston. Writing in 1953, H.D. Wendland pointed out that thirty years earlier the drift of Christian social thought had been away from eschatology. Christians had felt that their appropriate function was not to wait for the Kingdom of God, but to work for the improvement of human society themselves. Wendland went on to argue:

> Today we need to move in the opposite direction, away from a social ethic which has its roots in a secular, autonomous, idealistic, or humanistic outlook, away even from a "Christian sociology" back into the realm of eschatology. (17)

The Evanston theme was "Christ - the Hope of the World", and the eschatological note sounded in its social thought. It would be wrong to assume, however, that there was general agreement as to how the Kingdom of God relates to present society. There were those who stressed that the Kingdom was already realized. This view often accompanies an extreme form of the Lutheran "two-world" doctrine in which the saving work of Christ has to do with individual souls and the Kingdom, made up of such, is isolated from the concerns of this world. Certainly, when held alone, it is productive of an ethical escapism and a religious isolationism. At the opposite end of the scale there were those who considered the Kingdom of God to be a wholly future condition. This view, which issues in a world-forsaking attitude and an abandonment of social responsibility, was not influential at Evanston.

Far more significant was the view that the Kingdom of God is realizable within history and by human efforts. Ideas of this type had made their presence felt since the inception of the Life and Work Movement. Their tendency is to identify social improvements and legal reform with the doing of God's will. The weaknesses of this view are that it takes from Christianity the essential element of tension between what is and what is yet to be, and it naively assumes that the salvation of the world will be brought about by human efforts. Clearly, it does not pay enough attention to the power of evil in history.

Although agreement on eschatological emphases was not reached at Evanston, the point was made that social ethics, including those on race relations, must include an eschatological component. Only a balanced eschatology can lead men through the demonic ideologies of the day and can furnish a secure hope, in the light of which Christians will gain necessary insights into the complex problems caused by evil in the world and simultaneously find initiative and strength to play a responsible role in human affairs.

Finally, Evanston acknowledged the place of "ends" in social ethics and Oldham did not. The primary use of ends is seen in the concept inherited from the Amsterdam Assembly of the "Responsible Society". Amsterdam had developed it as an alternative in the sterile battle between the socialist and capitalist models. It was defined as follows:

> A responsible society is one where freedom is the freedom of men who acknowledge responsibility to justice and public order and where those who hold political authority or economic power are responsible for its exercise to God and the people whose welfare is affected by it. (18)

This concept influenced Christian thought on many aspects of society including those which had a bearing on race relations. A model for race relations, however, could not be formulated on the same lines. This was due to the particularity of race problems. In its efforts to outline such a model, Evanston did make some useful distinctions between integration, pluralism and segregation. (19) The latter implies involuntary or imposed separation on the assumption that racial groups should be kept apart. It usually takes the form of a carefully defined policy and is distinct from discrimination which is more a matter of individual behaviour, although in practice where there is segregation there is usually discrimination. Voluntary separation of groups is referred to as pluralism. This social policy assumes that racial differences should be recognized and accepted as desirable. If only as a temporary measure, groups should cultivate their distinctive differences without disadvantage to themselves or to the wider community. This form of separation sees the various groups in a given society as ranged horizontally alongside each other rather than placed above each other according to privilege, as is usually the case with segregation. It is noted that at the time of the Oxford Conference pluralism was widely held as the most appropriate solution of racial and ethnic problems, but that many former exponents of pluralism have now moved sharply towards the third option, that of integration. This model, sometimes alluded to as "the melting-pot model", allows for no separation or distinction between groups. Opportunities to make use of the resources of society are available equally to all. If there is discrimination it does not have a racial origin. Indeed, there are legal guarantees against racial and ethnic discrimination. This model, in theory at least, ensures that intergroup tensions are at a minimum. Although it is not easy to make a general conclusion as to which social "end" held sway at Evanston, it is probably correct to say that the idea of integration was the most influential.

Underlying this inconclusiveness was an even more fundamental matter which also had to be left undecided by the Second Assembly. This was the debate between the two ethical methods, one based on "ends" and the other on "inspiration". The Amsterdam Assembly saw this area of disagreement as "our deepest difference". The difficulty of achieving a consensus lay in the fact that the choice between the two ethical approaches was not simply a choice in a vacuum. The two are based on theological premises and each is firmly rooted in its own ecclesiastical traditions.

The "ethic of ends" is bound up with the concept of a natural law which operates with an ideal picture of man. Man is a creature capable of rational thought. By reason he knows that he has an eternal destiny. His reasoning ability itself is a pointer towards this conclusion. In the same way he knows that he is intended to live in society. He is able, by rational analysis, to gain a pattern of the ideal society. From this pattern he can derive norms to which a man may look for guidance when making a moral judgement in a specific set of circumstances. These norms give a clear indication of the way in which the various parts of society properly fit together. The Christian's obedience in society is to the norms with which his created reason, assisted, enhanced and enlightened by God's grace, has provided him.

The "ethic of inspiration", on the other hand, is based on a view of human nature which gives more weight to the fall of man and his consequent sinful nature. Any norms which such a man devised would certainly not be a guide for Christian conduct in society. Rather, the Christian ought to seek first to respond fully to the initiative of God in the hope that a proper relationship with God will be brought about. From this relationship alone spring the attitudes and insights necessary for living as a Christian in society. Those who follow this method give a central place to the Bible, because, for them, it is the primary source of our knowledge of God.

Edward Duff describes convincingly the depth of the conflict between the two methods.[20] We agree with Duff in his interpretation of the "responsible society" model as an instance of the tendency towards an "ethic of ends". To his examples of the tendency towards an "ethic of inspiration" at Evanston, we add one from the Resolution on Intergroup Relations. Speaking of the need to secure the franchise for all men, it describes the nature of the action required simply as:

> ... such action as, under God, they may be led to take ...[21]
> In spite of the inhibiting effect of the disagreement on ethical

method, Evanston did contribute to World Council thought on race relations. As we have noted, it drew together the main strands of that thought and thus formulated clearly, if generally, the Christian witness on the subject.

The task of the churches is made plain. They are to challenge the conscience of society both by their words and their way of life. In order to achieve this they must continually scrutinize themselves. The church must expect tension between itself and the society in which it belongs. This is especially true where a society gives formal acceptance to racial discrimination.

> The Church of Christ cannot approve of any law which discriminates on grounds of race, which restricts the opportunity of any person to acquire education to prepare himself for his vocation, to procure or to practice employment in his vocation, or in any other way curtails his exercise of full rights and responsibilities of citizenship and of sharing in the responsibilities and duties of government. (22)

Because of its divisive effects, race discrimination runs counter to the nature of the ecumenical movement and of the church.

> Physical separation within the Church on grounds of race is a denial of spiritual unity and of the brotherhood of man. (23)

The fundamental theological objection is as follows:

> Racial and ethnic fears, hates and prejudices are more than social problems with whose existence we must reckon; they are sins against God and His commandments that the gospel alone can cure. (24)

The findings of the Section were given added authority by Resolutions adopted by the whole Assembly. The first and most notable of these takes the form of a strongly worded definitive statement which epitomises the witness of the Evanston Assembly.

> The Second Assembly of the World Council of Churches declares its conviction that any form of segregation based on race, colour and ethnic origin is contrary to the Gospel, and is incompatible with the Christian doctrine of man and the nature of the Church of Christ. The Assembly urges the Churches within its membership to renounce all forms of segregation or discrimination and to work for their abolition within their own life and within society. (25)

The Resolutions also include a recommendation to the Central Committee that, in consultation with the I.M.C., it:

> ... make structural provision for an organization, preferably a department, giving assistance to the constituent Churches in their efforts to bring the gospel to bear more effectively upon relations between racial and ethnic groups.

We cannot agree with van der Bent, writing in 1973, that the Evanston statement is still the basis for the World Council's action. (26) On the other hand the significant contribution of Evanston to subsequent thought and action can not be denied.

Chapter II
POLICY AND ACTION - I: CONTACT, CONSULTATION AND STATEMENT

The Evanston Resolution, as we have seen, called upon the Central Committee to "make structural provision" for a organization which would exist for the purpose of fostering better race relations. Its primary task would be to give assistance to the member churches in their attempts to "bring the gospel to bear more effectively" upon relations between racial and ethnic groups. For six years following Evanston the plan was not put into effect. During that period it appeared in the Central Committee records under the heading: "Proposals which have been accepted by the Assembly or Central Committee but for which no financial provision has yet been made."

The Central Committee meeting three years after Evanston reviewed the situation and approved interim action on three points, to be undertaken by the Division of Ecumenical Action.(27) First, the services of a competent consultant were to be sought.(28) His task would be to help churches in areas of racial and ethnic tension to make their work more relevant and effective. The finance for such a consultant was to come from "means outside the normal sources of income". Secondly, a study was to be promoted of the biblical and theological bases of racial and ethnic relations. The phrasing of this point reveals a sense of uneasiness in the face of the variety of approaches within the World Council as regards theology and methods of biblical interpretation. Thirdly, the Divisional Committee was to be responsible for recommendations being brought to the Central Committee which gave continued expression to the concern for racial and ethnic relations during the period 1961 to 1967.

The following year, 1958, saw no diminution of concern. The Commission of the Churches on International Affairs examined the situation in South Africa and the (then) Federation of Rhodesia and Nyasaland. Studies within the Rapid Social Change programme embraced race and problems related to it in a report on South Africa, in a study conference in the Copperbelt of the (then) Northern Rhodesia, and in a consultation in Indonesia which discussed "Caste in Church and Nation". The Central Committee noted the "recent tragic developments in Ceylon", which underlined the urgent need for the help which a field consultant could give.(29)

The financial support needed for such an appointment had still to be found. In 1959 the same state of affairs prevailed. The chairman, however, was able to report one hopeful development. A generous grant from a private individual had made possible a two month study of the experiences of American churches in dealing with situations of racial tension. The Rev. Daisuke Kitagawa was released from the Rapid Social Change study in order to carry out the enquiry. It was hoped that his findings would be useful to churches outside the United States which faced similar problems. The Finance Committee admitted the failure of efforts made since Evanston to secure gifts to make possible the implementation of the measures called for in the Assembly Resolution. It went on to recommend the inclusion in the general budget after the Third Assembly of a sum for a Secretariat for Inter-Group Relations.(30) In 1960 the <u>Secretariat for Racial and Ethnic Relations</u> was established within the Department on Church and Society under the leadership of Daisuke Kitagawa.

The delay in reaching this point and the scaling down of the Evanston preference for a whole department are not wholly explicable in financial terms. A factor which contributed to the delay was the exaggerated confidence which the World Council placed in the efficacy of its statements. More important than this was the lack of a clear conception of the objectives and methods of the Secretariat. While the World Council was totally convinced of the importance of race relations for the health of society at large, it was far from sure as to how best to set about the task of understanding and improving such relations.

This uncertainty is clear in the proposals made to the Third Assembly by a Consultation on Racial and Ethnic Relations which met in Geneva in April 1961 to make recommendations concerning the work of the Secretariat. The Consultation echoed the feeling that was present in the preparatory work for Evanston and later expressed in the 1956 Central Committee meeting. It stated that a change of method was necessary because the situation of the churches had changed.

> The enunciation of policies against segregation and discrimination is not enough in the current situation. Events force the churches to take a stand on concrete and complex situations.

It felt that the principles stated by Evanston were valid, useful and, for present purposes, sufficient. But the forthcoming Third Assembly ought to recognize that the churches have:

> ... not acted dynamically enough since the Evanston Assembly for the elimination of segregation in the churches and in society.(31)

The Consultation considered the church as "watchman" and "prophetic voice" and asked if these functions could be not only negative, against segregation and discrimination, but also positive, proclaiming a goal for race relations such as integration or the multi-racial society. It continued:

> Can the church stand behind such announced social goals, and if so, what weight of theological conviction may it give to its position? This is at root to raise the basic question whether the Christian understanding of "race" is such that ultimate theological categories can be directly applied to the question of race relations, or whether these relationships must be treated in different ways, relative to the demands of the Gospel upon specific situations.(32)

Once again, in attempting to address itself to a particular social problem, the World Council found itself faced with the unresolved tension between an "ethic of ends" and an "ethic of inspiration". The suggestion in the above passage is that general principles, derived from predetermined social goals and universally applicable, are of limited use in an attempt to frame a Christian racial policy. There is an awareness of the highly specific nature of racial problems and a hint that ethical method may have to be changed as a result. There is no actual problem which may be called "the racial problem". There are only many varied problem situations in which relationships are sullied between individuals and groups of different race. The starting point may have to be, not the formulation of general principles, but a painstaking empirical analysis of each situation. The expectations, then, will be no longer in terms of ultimate goals. Instead, Christian thinking on race relations will have as its aim the selection of that combination of options from among many others, which seems to make possible a more Christian state of affairs. Precisely what content is given to the idea "more Christian", whether it be explained in terms of love, justice or some other norm, is an open question. What is clear is that we shall not be dealing in absolutes so much as in relativities. Unfortunately the proposals of the Consultation did not press the matter as far as we have done. They only stated the alternative approaches and left the problem of ethical method unresolved. The problem was to persist.

The New Delhi Assembly in 1961 welcomed the establishment of the Secretariat. In a resolution it called the attention of the member churches to the mounting racial and ethnic tensions which accompanied both rapid social change and the struggle for social justice in many areas. (33) It expressed gratitude for the courage and witness of individuals and groups who were struggling to uphold Christian witness and unity in racially troubled areas. Gratitude was also expressed for the similar witness of those non-Christians who were exercising leadership in the struggle for human rights in a spirit of forgiveness and non-violence. This point is noteworthy because it reveals the growing secular interest of the World Council. It shows a strong sympathy with those who are working for a more just society but who may have no connection whatsoever with the church - and this in a resolution, the World Council's strongest form of utterance. The scope of its social concern is extending the major interests of the World Council beyond the borders of the institutional church and even beyond what may be thought of as distinctively Christian. An ecclesiology seems to be emerging in which the generally accepted boundaries between the church and the world are blurred.

The Resolution reminded the churches of the Evanston declaration and urged them to act more resolutely than before in carrying out its terms. It also urged them to give their support to the development of the programme of the Secretariat.

An outline of that programme, drawn substantially from the proposals of the Special Consultation held in Geneva earlier that year, was recommended in the report of the Committee on the Department on Church and Society. (34) It reveals some doubt as to the adequacy of current theological categories when related to the precise understanding seen to be required of each problem situation. Four areas of study were suggested. First, an analysis must be made from a Christian perspective of the causes and consequences of racial tension in society. Secondly, the meaning of "race" must be examined and its significance gauged in terms of such fundamental Christian doctrines as those of man, creation, salvation and the church. Reciprocally, the categories of Christian theology must be questioned as to their adequacy in dealing with racial problems. Thirdly, a study should be made of the effect of racial tensions on political, economic and social life in order to ascertain appropriate Christian action and to guide the local congregation in its work as an agent for reconciliation in society. Finally, non-violence must be evaluated as a possible Christian method of achieving moral and structural change in segregated societies.

Some operative principles were enunciated. The Secretariat must serve the World Council and the member churches by stimulating their thought and action on racial and ethnic matters. The unity of racial and ethnic groups within the churches is to be promoted. (35) The Secretariat is to conduct itself as a servant of the churches and other Christian organizations in the various countries. Ideally the churches should first request its service, but it may at times be necessary for the Secretariat itself to initiate specific programmes. In these cases the full support of the churches concerned should be secured.

Finally, eight lines of action were recommended. Emphasis falls heavily on study and the communication of ideas. Ecumenical studies are to be undertaken in the four areas outlined above. The attention of the Secretariat is to be focussed largely upon particular instances of tension in the various countries. Appropriate action is the organization of international and regional conferences and consultations, and the exchange of competent personnel and useful information. Existing programmes and facilities are to be used as fully as possible and co-operation is to be achieved with churches, mission agencies and the various departments of the World Council itself, especially the Division of World Mission and Evangelism.

Thus the direction to be taken by the Secretariat was indicated, and the nature of its work prescribed. As well as study projects, it was committed to a policy of <u>contact, consultation</u> and <u>statement.</u> In its Resolution, New Delhi expressed gratitude for those churches which, though divided by different approaches to the question of race relations, were yet willing to meet with each other and to enter into dialogue to the end that they might "discover together the will of God for their common witness to Christ in society". (36) <u>Contact</u> between churches was not only an expedient policy. It was a principle at the heart of ecumenism itself. The Geneva Consultation was explicit on the connection between local and ecumenical issues. In its service to the churches the Secretariat should constantly remind them that the power of reconciliation is in Jesus Christ and the fellowship of his church.

> Specifically, this will mean helping to foster a helpful interaction between purely local situations and broader ecumenical relations and perspectives. (37)

In its section on Witness, New Delhi expressed its conviction that contact between individuals, groups and institutions was fundamental to the nature of the church and the very purpose of God.

> The gathering of the Church by Jesus Christ in every age demonstrates the loving purpose of God to draw men out of isolation and sinful separation into a community of brothers with a common Father, God himself .... By the Spirit the Church is moved to the service of neighbour without distinction or discrimination. Through his Church God witnesses to his purpose to gather all nations, peoples and tongues, all sorts and conditions of men into his city.(38)

Within this contact, ecumenical study on racial questions was to take place. The main method of study was to be that of <u>consultation</u>. Included under this heading were the "field visits" undertaken by the Staff of the Secretariat, as well as national and international conferences to which representatives of the member churches and experts in the field of racial and ethnic relations would be invited. It was hoped that such activities would involve a combination of insights of theology, the social sciences, social work and the pastoral ministry. While the Committee on Techniques and Methods of Ecumenical Study on Social Questions could recommend such consultations as the best technique known at the time, it was not convinced that it was an entirely satisfactory method. The committee recommended that the search for more effective methods be continued.

The aim of many ecumenical assemblies, studies and consultations was the issuing of a <u>statement</u>, by which findings and areements would be reinforced and publicized. It seems to have been assumed that words have a certain intrinsic power to achieve the end of which they speak. It was hoped that the united Christian source of a statement would lend its message added moral authority and thus help it to achieve the desired effect. That effect was the changing of men's minds and attitudes by moral persuasion and community pressure.

The policy of contact, consultation and statement underwent its acid test in the period leading up to the New Delhi Assembly. Probably the most notable ecumenical event of the year, the <u>Cottesloe Consultation</u>, was convened in Johannesburg in December 1960. It provides us with the paradigm case of the application of the policy which we have been discussing. Therefore, we shall examine it at some length. The disappointing repercussions which dashed the high hopes attending the consultation must account in part for the hesitance of New Delhi towards the policy which seemed the best available at the time.

The cruciality of the South African case lay in the fact that Christianity had played a leading historical role there. The dominant white group claimed to uphold a Christian civilization. In a census in 1960, seventy-two per cent of a population torn by racial tension professed to be Christians. It had long been felt in the World Council that the South African churches were isolated from the main stream of ecumenical influence. The divisions between races and the consequent deleterious effects on all aspects of society including the life of the church were matters of deep concern. The disturbances early in 1960 which led to the tragedy at Sharpeville (39) underlined the explosive potentialities of a situation fraught with racial discrimination and reinforced by a government policy of strict segregation. In April, the Anglican Archbishop of Cape Town stated that the events at Sharpeville had confronted the church in South Africa with the gravest crisis in its history. It was, he said, condemning itself to extinction unless it publicly repudiated both the doctrine and the practice of apartheid. (40) He urged the Dutch Reformed Churches to identify themselves with this attitude and requested that the World Council of Churches send a fact finding group to investigate the situation.

The Dutch Reformed Churches reacted strongly. In a letter to the World Council the Nederduitse Gereformeende Kerk of the Transvaal denied "... a few bishops the right to demand for themselves a monopoly over South Africa's Christian conscience".(41) Together with its sister church in the Cape, it said that it would welcome a visit by an investigatory team from the World Council. In response Dr. Robert Bilheimer, director of the Division of Studies and an Associate General Secretary, visited South Africa. After discussion between him and leaders of the eight member churches there it was agreed that the World Council would undertake to arrange for a consultation for the purpose of finding together some means of reconciliation between both churches and racial groups.

The consultation was to be inter-racial and the World Council delegation itself was to include people of various races. The frustrated intention of the Central Committee to send such a delegation to South Africa ten years earlier was to be fulfilled (see page 12). It was understood that participations would represent widely differing convictions. The preparatory documents of the various churches revealed strong disagreements as to the causes of the tension which had led to the Sharpeville incident. The official statement noted the wide range of attitudes towards apartheid at the Consultation. Various degrees of approval and disapproval were expressed.

It was known that advice from outside South Africa was habitually met with strong resentment. On account of this the World Council made it clear to the South African member churches that the purpose of the consultation would not be to convert one another nor "to attempt to enforce convictions which have been crystallized in ecumenical debate". Rather they should endeavour to enter into a deeper fellowship with one another and together seek the guidance of God in achieving a better understanding of his purpose in South Africa.(42) This was also in keeping with the constitution of the World Council in which the autonomy of the member churches is protected.

The venue was the Cottesloe residence of the University of the Witwatersrand. The World Council sent a six man delegation headed by Dr. Franklin Clark Fry, who was also chairman of the meetings. Each of the eight member churches in South Africa sent ten delegates. During the week of meetings a profound sense of community was experienced by those present. Worship and Bible study were part of the proceedings.

At the outset Dr. Fry made it known that the planning committee had made no advance provision for the drafting of a statement. The meeting must itself decide whether or not it wished to take such a step. After three days of discussion the delegates expressed their wish for a statement. There can be no doubt, in the light of its own policy, that the World Council was highly gratified by this decision.

As with all other decisions, each paragraph of the statement needed the approval of eighty per cent of the participants. This requirement ensured that substantial majorities from each of the major confessional and racial groups represented would be in support of decisions. It was hoped that the authoritative nature of the statement would be assured by this numerical and representative majority. The statement as a whole is more moderate than similar ecumenical statements. In its South African context, however, it was a dramatic document which called for profound changes in social and political patterns.

Admitting that they proceeded from divergent views, the delegates agreed that they were able to make some general affirmations concerning human need and justice as these affect relations between the races. The church, by its nature, is called to minister to human need as it manifests itself in both individuals and groups. It must be "deeply concerned" with the welfare of people and insist "that all be done with justice". Finally it was agreed that Scripture is the supreme guide in any consideration of the complex of factors which affect the life of a people.

> ... the Church must proclaim that the final criterion of all social and political action is the principles of Scripture regarding the realization for all men of a life worthy of their God-given vocation. (43)

This affirmation is noteworthy for two reasons. First, it echoes the confidence of those in ecumenical circles who had for long looked to Scripture as the starting point for Christian social ethics. (44) Secondly, there was no common interpretation of Scripture. Indeed there was strong disagreement between the English and the Afrikaans speaking churches as to the "principles of Scripture" which applied to race relations.

Some of the pronouncements are of a mainly religious nature, but in places even these were highly controversial in the South African context. One point, for example, affirms the unity between Christians and on this ground condemns racial exclusiveness within the church.

> No-one who believes in Jesus Christ may be excluded from any church on the grounds of his colour or race. The spiritual unity among all men who are in Christ must find visible expression in acts of common worship and witness, and in fellowship and consultation on matters of common concern. (45)

On practical religious issues it is declared that the church has the duty and right to proclaim the gospel to whomever it will, and in whatever circumstances. Any legislation which limits this freedom is regarded as unacceptable. In the interests of freedom of worship, the state is urged to allow the provision of "adequate and convenient facilities" for non-white people to worship in urban areas. For the same reason it is suggested that white congregations in those areas make their own buildings available for non-whites to use for worship. A glaring omission in this section is that white congregations are in no way encouraged to share their religious activities with people of other races.

Other pronouncements reveal a strong social concern. These angered many white church members, who felt that the church had no right in this area and should restrict itself to the "spiritual sphere". The statement was especially critical of African wage levels and labour conditions. The migrant labour system was condemned as having a disintegrating effect on African family life and as such constituting a threat to social stability. "Concerted action" was called for to remedy "this grave situation".

Probably the most contentious proposal of all, and the one with the most far-reaching implications for the country, was that which dealt with the rights of property ownership and of concomitant political participation.

> It is our conviction that the right to own land wherever he is domiciled, and to participate in the government of his country, is part of the dignity of the adult man, and for this reason a policy which permanently denies to non-white people the right of collaboration in the government of the country of which they are citizens cannot be justified. (46)

The mode of participation envisaged is left open. If an attempt had been made to outline specific details it is highly unlikely that agreement would have been reached.

Finally, with a view to an increase in mutual understanding between the churches, a request was made for the exchange of official publications between the member churches. Also, when making approaches to the government, churches should keep each other fully informed of their procedures. A strong call was made that in such approaches the delegations be "combined if possible", and a weaker call that they be "multi-racial where appropriate". A recommendation urged that whenever a church felt bound to criticize another church, or church leader, it should take the initiative in seeking prior consultation with the party in question before making any public statement.

At first it seemed that at least one objective of the Consultation had been realized, namely the reconciliation of the Anglican and Dutch Reformed Churches. The reaction of the Dutch Reformed Churches, however, was to dash all hopes of success in terms of improved ecumenical contact. Simultaneous with the Consultation statement they issued statements of their own. The delegations of the Nederduitse Gereformeerde Churches of the Cape and Trasvaal stated their belief that:

> ... a policy of differentiation can be defended from the Christian point of view, that it provides the only realistic solution to the problems of race relations and is therefore in the best interests of the various population groups. (47)

The statement of the Nederduitsch Hervormde delegates was more strongly worded. For them, "separate development" was "the only just solution of our racial problems", integration in any form was rejected, and some Cottesloe declarations were too far-reaching to be supported.

A storm broke loose in the Afrikaans speaking churches. The prime minister intervened and, in his new year message for 1961, said that any form of political multi-racialism or partnership would ultimately deprive the white man of his "rightful heritage". He challenged the Dutch Reformed delegates to formulate a moral basis for such policies. He argued that the delegates were expressing their own private views and that the churches were yet to speak through their synods. This speech gained enthusiastic support in the Afrikaans language press. The synods followed these promptings and, by October 1961, the three Dutch Reformed Churches had voted to withdraw from membership of the World Council. The main grounds given for the decisions were that the Cottesloe findings were an embarrassment to the government and at variance with the policy of the church - this latter despite the earlier acknowledgement by the two Nederduitse Gereformeerde Churches that the Cottesloe statement flowed in the main from memoranda prepared beforehand by about fifty professors, ministers and missionaries of their churches.

Elfriede Strassberger poses the question of whether Cottesloe marked the end of hopes raised by a decade full of promise for ecumenical relations in South Africa, or whether it was

> ... in some mysterious way ... the beginning of a genuine road leading to deeper relationships between Christian Churches in South Africa, after a consultation which brought out the skeletons in the cupboards, but which pointed the way to renewal. (48)

She offers no clear aswer, but seems to suggest that Cottesloe was not only a peak achievement in itself in terms of the deep Christian fellowship and mutual understanding experienced by the delegates, but that it gave rise to new and unanticipated departures in ecumenical progress. It is true that a small number of ecumenical study groups was formed and that such ventures as the Christian Institute and the dissenting Christian periodical Pro Veritate were launched. These, however, are minor achievements in comparison with the hopes for improved inter-church and inter-racial relations which attended Cottesloe. Roger Lloyd's assessment is near the truth when he says that, despite its many valuable findings, Cottesloe's long-term effect was one of failure. (49)

The dynamics of the World Council policy lay in the tension between the will for social justice and the desire for Christian unity. This tension had long been felt by the South African churches. As early as 1953 a Dutch Reformed delegate to the Central Committee meeting at which a stong resolution condemning racial segregation was adopted expressed the feeling of "the last drop of blood being squeezed out of us". (50) After Cottesloe the tension was broken. It had not proved to be creative.

The Secretariat for Racial and Ethnic Relations had only just been established. Its programme was yet to be ratified by the Third Assembly. Yet the policy which it was to follow had already proved to be inadequate in a paradigm case. A question mark stood not only against the policy but also against the social philosophy from which it sprang.

In its Message to Christians in South Africa, the <u>New Delhi Assembly</u> expressed its regret at the withdrawal of the Dutch Reformed Churches. In contrast it rejoiced that twenty-three churches had joined the World Council at the Assembly, eleven of them from Africa. South African Christians were reminded of and urged to adhere to the affirmations of Cottesloe concerning the supra-racial character of the church and of the Christian faith. The theme of the Assembly was "Jesus Christ, the Light of the World". With this was contrasted the darkness of the world to which racial strife contributed. Encouragement was given to Christians everywhere, but particularly in South Africa, who were struggling and suffering for the elimination of racial segregation or discrimination. It was hoped that the church would be increasingly creative and constructive in these concerns.

The Central Committee meeting in 1963, held in Rochester, New York, coincided with the march on Washington organized by civil rights groups. Its statement on racial and ethnic tensions reveals the general feeling that the struggle was approaching its climax. Shame is expressed at the hesitation, and even the efforts "on the wrong side" of the struggle, of some Christians. Those involved in the contemporary non-violent action for justice were accorded "the wholehearted support" of the meeting. The churches in the United States were urged to redouble their efforts in their ministry of reconciliation with relation to the particular problem situations in that country. An even larger section dealing specifically with South Africa indicates that the shockwaves from Cottesloe and its aftermath were still felt with great intensity in the World Council. The statement recognizes that at Cottesloe church leaders had shown a way of reversing the trend towards increased conflict, but that this way had not been followed.

> The white Christians in the Republic must reconsider the way the churches have gone since then. They are urged to a determination to repudiate - by deeds as well as words - all that weakens their witness to Christ in whom all men are one. (51)

The ecumenical policy of contact is translated into a political usage.

> Isolation will lead to conflict; communication is the prerequisite of peace. (52)

For this reason Christians outside South Africa are to work to inform world opinion of the crisis in that country. They must urge the government of the Republic to re-establish contact with the African, Coloured and Indian communities and to reverse quickly the political trend which deprives these people of their political, civil and economic rights.

Three points emerge in this statement which hint at the beginnings of a change of course in World Council thinking on racial problems. The first of these concerns economic involvement. Governments are warned that by maintaining selfish national interests in South Africa they may do much to defer the realization of racial justice in that country. Secondly, Christians must do all in their power to show their care for the victims of discrimination and to relieve the needs of refugees from South Africa. This indicates that the World Council was beginning to look for appropriate means of action beyond the mainly ecclesiastical limits to which it had usually confined itself. (53) Clearly the World Council was beginning to see the secular sphere as its rightful field of action. Thirdly, there is a new note of pessimism with regard to constitutional and legal methods of effecting change in some situations. It is acknowledged that the majority of black South Africans had abandoned hope of an "internal solution". They had begun to look to an initiative from outside the country to bring about a just solution to their problems. The form of this initiative is not specified in the statement.

The pessimistic note had grown in volume by the time of the Consultation held in Kitwe, Zambia in 1964. The meetings were convened by the Department on Church and Society in co-operation with the South African Institute of Race Relations and the Mindolo Ecumenical Foundation whose headquarters were the venue. Participants did not come as representatives of churches or other organizations, but as individuals with a concern for "Christian Practice and Desirable Action in Social Change and Race Relations", which was the theme of the meetings. The participants did represent a wide variety of backgrounds. Eduardo Mondlane and other African nationalists took part for the first time in a meeting sponsored by the World Council of Churches. Dutch Reformed members from South Africa were also present.(54)

The pessimism of which we speak was by no means the only mood which coloured the thinking at Mindolo. Many of the participants from the newly independent African countries brought with them an almost utopian optimism. In his address, D.A. Etheredge sounded a warning.

> Africans will need to be rescued from the disillusionment which inevitably follows wild hopes of a Utopia just around the corner.(55)

The experience of both national independence and many new ecclesiastical and political ventures in Africa had given rise to high hopes for social justice and progress, political solidarity and Christian unity. The Organization of African Unity, the All Africa Youth Assembly and the All Africa Conference of Churches had only just been established. This confident mood was to highlight the plight of those Africans who had no say whatsoever in their own affairs and who in no way shared the new-found sense of dignity and self-determination. The contrasting pessimism was related to the marked lack of success which had attended the ecumenical method of social action as well as other legal and constitutional methods to effect change in Southern Africa.

The Consultation was conscious of the need to go beyond what had been stated at Evanston, Cottesloe and New Delhi. These had registered concern and had stated Christian conviction clearly. The "increasing anger and violence" which race problems produced were now acknowledged as part of the given context in which decisions had to be made. The question of means of bringing about social change was raised more emphatically at this than at any previous ecumenical gathering. Professor Z.K.Matthews, a black South African and a member of the World Council staff at the time, gave a key address entitled "The Road from Non-Violence to Violence". He outlined the historical succession of events which had increased the oppression of the Africans in South Africa and described how all attempts to reverse the trend by legal and constitutional means had failed. The Africans were a loyal and law-abiding people. Their leaders had stood by the policy of non-violence and had hoped by that means to achieve co-operation between black and white on the basis of equal opportunity. Their efforts had been in vain and their methods had been discredited. They were in danger of being replaced by others who were willing to employ more violent means. In short, violence was fast gaining ground as a possible and a just option. Most African leaders were very reluctant to think in this direction and their object most certainly was not the destruction of the state. Nor was it their ambition to drive out the white man in accordance with the cry: "Africa for the Africans". What they wanted was participation in a state which would have as its aim a just social and political system. Past events and present attitudes among white people give strong support to those who argue that illegal and violent means are the only way open to the black man who is serious in his commitment to change. Matthews' point is clear in the following extract:

> The intransigence on the white side of the colour line is being met with similar intransigence on the black side of the colour line. Unable to get the ear of public authorities in their own countries, the non-white have begun to look beyond their own borders for inspiration, guidance and direction. Already events in other parts of the continent of Africa are having a tremendous impact on the man-in-the-street in South Africa. Already he sees that people in other territories in Africa are on the march towards independence, some of them obtaining their independence by peaceful methods, while others have had to fight to gain their freedom. It is not surprising that he says to himself, "if we cannot achieve our freedom by peaceful means, we may have to resort to other methods". The question at the moment is not whether the latter methods will succeed, but whether they begin to appear to the African in South Africa as the only methods open to him. (56)

Mindolo's condsideration of violent methods was far from irresponsible It stands well within the "just war" tradition in that it asks searching questions, based on an understanding of violence and its consequences, of those who intend to embark on such a course. First, it asks whether they have exhausted all possibilities of non-violent action. The second question concerns the purity of their motives and asks whether they have done all in their power to rid themselves of hatred, bitterness and a spirit of revenge. They are also required to instil in their followers a sense of responsibility for the welfare of the whole population. The self-perpetuating nature of violence is recognized in the third question which asks leaders whether they have adequate safeguards to ensure that their strategy of violence, once embarked upon, will not result in uncontrolled mob violence.(57)

The role of the church in the face of the increasing urgency of racial tension was pointed out. In economic matters it must constantly remind the relevant authorities of the immorality of "a dual pattern of economic life". Great inequalities of wealth and income between racial groups and the selfish possession by a minority racial group of overwhelming economic power over a majority racial group are "repugnant to the Christian conscience". The victims of these economic injustices look to the church to secure relief from their grievances, but usually in vain. There is already much disillusionment with Christianity and many are seeking relief elsewhere. Churches must, therefore, not only speak out against economic injustice, they must also set an example in their own institutional life and support "every movement leading to the improvement of economic conditions for the African". Christians should work to remove obstacles in the way of African businessmen and, in particular, they should "persuade governments and private enterprises to make capital and credit facilities at reasonable interest available on a considerable scale." (58)

> The "Call to Churches and Christians", in general, is to: ... a sincere recognition and confession of their guilt in a situation for which they have long been responsible ...

The main areas of guilt which, if corrected, could make way for the discovery of new avenues of witness, service and reconciliation, are given as follows:

> ... the gulf of sinful silence when there was urgent need to speak both in prophecy and reconciliation, of lack of identification with the suffering and the oppressed, of indifference and unwillingness to become involved, of lack of real fellowship among Christians, and of neglect of duty in the education of the laity through proclamation and instruction. (59)

Clearly Mindolo had concern for the life of the church and for its increased effectiveness in witness. Equally clearly, it indicated that the way to achieve that end lay in the increased involvement of the church in secular affairs. A more overt stance must be adopted by the church in the economic, social and political spheres.

Daisuke Kitagawa, who had left the Secretariat on Racial and Ethnic Relations in 1963, returned to be chairman of the Mindolo Consultation. The method with which he and the Secretariat had operated was given its fullest expression at Cottesloe and at Mindolo. The major advantage of the former over the latter consultation, from an ecumenical viewpoint, was that its participants were the official representatives of member churches. Mindolo, on the other hand, could boast that its membership and its interests were international whereas Cottesloe's concern was for one country and its participants were nearly all South African.

On both occasions the principles of contact and consultation had been employed and found wanting. In the case of Cottesloe, as we have seen, the results were disappointing, although it is only fair to add that no other method would have been assured of success in the circumstances. The Mindolo Consultation itself was valuable and marked the high point of the Secretariat's activites. The topics which preoccupied the Consultation and more especially the action which was envisaged, however, were beyond the scope of the Secretariat. Not only was its budget small, but its programme was suited mainly to limited studies with the purpose of providing useful information to churches in areas of racial tension. The Secretariat was designed both to organise consultations and to function as a consultant itself. Those who shaped the Secretariat seem to have had in mind that it be a service on racial matters for member churches. Kitagawa himself was afraid that the Secretariat might simply duplicate work which was already being done by other agencies, but felt that the World Council did have a unique contribution to make. From its universal perspective it could help churches to locate their problems. With this in mind he saw the work of the Secretariat as being:

> ... to engage the member churches in a serious study first to put their finger on the question itself and then to find an adequate solution to it. (60)

In his function as a consultant, Kitagawa carried out a number of field studies. Reference has already been made to his earlier visit to the United States. He also visited Great Britain where he examined the effects of the influx of large numbers of West Indian, Pakistani and Indian immigrants, and the Copperbelt area of Northern Rhodesia soon before that country was to become the independent Zambia. The friction between Tamil and Sinhalese groups in Ceylon was also studied. In each case the major part of the information seems to have been gained in interviews based on elaborate questionaires. In keeping with its primary interest in the member churches, as opposed to society at large, most of the questions seem to have been addressed to church leaders and members about church concerns. The findings of these studies were tabulated in the Secretariat's main organ of communication, a mimeographed periodical entitled Race Relations in Ecumenical Perspective. Circulation was limited to those known to be interested and it was hoped that information from one problem situation would provide those involved in similar situations elsewhere with new insights. The accounts were largely factual and little or no attempt was made to point out likely solutions. The report on Ceylon, for example, supplied details of population, educational levels, religious affiliations, historical background, "Christian Actions so far Taken", "Christian Contributions Envisaged" and difficulties facing the Christian community. Possible lines of action to be pursued were alluded to only in the most general terms. (61) It seems that Kitagawa simply continued to follow the pattern which had been envisaged for a World Council consultant on race relations before the establishment of the Secretariat. Basing his ideas on the advice of J. Oscar Lee, Kitagawa stated that the consultant should not be an "expert" who intrudes on situations and provides the answers for the local community, and that he should not set about organizing a crusade to wipe out all racial tensions. He should rather be:

> ... a catalytic agent who helps Christians under racial tensions to mobilize all the resources at their disposal to gain insight into their own problem, to grasp its meaning for themselves. To this end he will be more likely than not promoting an "action-research" (note: <u>not</u> conducting it himself) in each area where his service is requested to be undertaken by Christians of that area.(62)

The function of the Secretariat, then, may be characterized by the term "diagnostic". It helped people to identify the trouble and its sources, to understand it as far as possible and to gain some inchoate insights into what might be done to remedy the situation.

The scope of the Secretariat's interest did go beyond matters directly affecting the life of the churches and their relation to the ecumenical movement, but there can be no doubt that these were by far its main concerns. The theological and institutional question of <u>racial churches</u>, for instance, exercised the Secretariat. Kitagawa's argument in this regard was that a racially organized denomination or confession infringed the ecumenical principle of "all in each place". The question of a racially organized local congregation could not be dealt with so easily. For practical reasons, such as hearing and understanding in one's own language and thought forms, it might be preferable that people meet with those of their own cultural or racial group. In a pluralistic society, however, there are reasons other than these to consider. The choice for the church must be whether it aims to provide its members with a comfortable, familiar environment or to relate the life of the congregation to the pluralistic society in which it has its place. Kitagawa advocates the latter alternative as the context in which the living Word of God might be heard and the congregational life be meaningful because it embraces the whole of life. In the end congregations organized on a racial basis, however much may be said for them, infringe basic ecumenical principles.(63)

Pastoral matters also fell within the interest of the Secretariat. One example is that of <u>interracial marriage.</u> The New Delhi Assembly had specified that this was an issue to which the Secretariat should give its attention and it became a recurrent topic. No progress was made, however, beyond the Evanston statement. There it was affirmed that neither justification for nor condemnation of such marriage could be found in the Bible, that the church could not approve any law against it, but that ministers of the church had a special duty in preparing couples planning to undertake interracial marriage. Its potential richness should be made known but also, given the racial attitudes of many societies, the probability of painful consequences. Cottesloe was more hesitant. Such marriages, it agreed, were not prohibited by Scripture, but social factors made them inadvisable. Mindolo, with its emphasis on change in society acknowledged that painful forms of social ostracism aften followed interracial marriage. The task of the church, therefore, was to educate public opinion and to create a "climate of acceptance" in the community for interracial families.

A view widely held in World Council social thinking was that
study and action should be held together. At New Delhi the following recommendation was made on methods of study on social questions:

> The Committee strongly endorses the increasing emphasis on the inter-relation between 'study' and 'action' and expresses the hope that in the post-New Delhi period this trend will become more widespread. (64)

Kitagawa admitted that in his six-year period of service on the staff of the World Council he had learned that action and study must be inseparably linked.

> Action preceded by no study is often misguided, while study followed by no action is obviously fruitless. (65)

It was not always clear, however, to what extent "study" was thought to be an act in itself and therefore to include "action". The programme of the Secretariat was heavily biased towards study. The aim was primarily to understand problems, to provide information on them and thereby to change people's minds. If Kitagawa consciously held "study" and "action" apart as two related but distinct concepts, as the above quotation suggests, then he must have been disappointed with the activity of the Secretariat. It was involved in little, if any, action per se which went beyond study. It seems that those who shaped the programme of the Secretariat, including Kitagawa himself, were influenced, wittingly or unwittingly, by the assumption that to study a problem was to act in an appropriate way. This "action-research" seems to have been the method which the World Council saw as its proper response to situations of racial tension. A succint expression of the assumptions behind such an approach was given by Paul Abrecht at the 1959 meeting of the Central Committee. Answering those who wanted certain findings to be transmitted into action he said:

> ... the formulation and spread of ideas are action ... (66)

This way of thinking was to face a strong challenge. A call of growing intensity was being made for the kind of action which had as its aim the changing, rather than the understanding alone, of unjust societies . This call was made loudly at Mindolo and gained the support of the Executive Committee which met later in 1964 at Tutzing, West Germany.

Chapter III

NEW DIRECTIONS IN THE SOCIAL THOUGHT OF THE WORLD COUNCIL OF CHURCHES

At New Delhi it was officially recognized that a more adequate basis for Christian social thought was required. Such were the changes in the world and in the patterns of society to which the Christian message had to relate that a simple modernization of previously used methods of thought would not suffice. New categories must be sought with which to understand the new world situation. Only when these began to emerge could the church relate properly to the world. The sense of urgency which accompanied this conviction was a correlate of the widespread feeling that the present was largely discontinuous with the past. The state of affairs at hand and the problems arising from it were emphatically new.

Nowhere did the need for a new way of thinking emerge more strongly than in the Rapid Social Change study which took place under the auspices of the Department on Church and Society between 1955 and 1961. The task of that study was to assess the developments in those parts of the world in which there was a clear movement from old to new forms of life in society. The study was particularly concerned with those countries which had recently been undergoing decolonization. Many of these countries had come within the province of the International Missionary Council rather than of the World Council. Indeed, in the period between the First and Second Assemblies, few member churches belonged to those areas. Western Christians can not be accused of having had no concern for the process of decolonization and the far-reaching political and social changes that ensued. They did not, however, share the sense of urgency which characterized the attitudes of those actually involved in the changes, which had been increasing in momentum since the close of the Second World War.

The Ecumenical Study Conference in Lucknow, India, in 1952, was one of the first serious attempts made by the World Council to come to grips with "the social revolution". The facts of the situation in East Asia together with the challenge of communism, which appeared to many to offer thought forms more relevant to the needs of that situation, aroused the World Council to seek a constructive attitude of its own. The Lucknow report expresses the desire that "a positive programme for social justice" be found. Social justice is described as:

> ... the development of social conditions in which human dignity and freedom can find their expression as befits the nature and destiny of man as a child of God.(67)

Out of the issues raised at Lucknow, the Rapid Social Change study developed. In accordance with the theme: "The Common Christian Responsibility Toward Areas of Rapid Social Change", field studies were undertaken and thereby the links between the World Council and churches

35

and missions in Africa, Asia, Latin America and the Middle East were considerably strengthened. (68) One result of the study was the increase in numbers of 'younger churches' which joined the World Council. Their voice was now heard from within. Their opinions and attitudes became increasingly influential. The World Council was determined that their contribution should be as effective as possible. Non-Western participation was encouraged at all levels. In leadership and in decision-making processes the new presence was strongly felt.

A second consequence was that the World Council now had within its own constituency a vocal and vigorous source self-criticism. Many of the assumptions with which it had previously operated in its social thought were shaken. Social change had been conceived of in terms of gradual development. Now it was clear that, in the face of the rapid dissolution of the old social structures and customs, the need was for political and social systems which would support development of a new and rapid kind. The Western churches were made aware of the colouring of their social ethics by the idea of Christendom. In spite of their interest in secularization, they still tended to think of society as a kind of unity in which the permeating influences of Christian values and institutions were strong. Christian social thought in the new nations operated with concepts of society as pluralistic. The Christian contribution to social ethics in this context was one among many and was characterized by its striving for the promotion of human values. Nationalism was also viewed in a new light. Ecumenical thought had previously displayed a highly critical attitude towards nationalism. Had it not contributed towards hostility between nations in the West? Attention was now directed towards:

> ... a different kind of nationalism in a different phase of history in the areas of rapid social change ... (69)

Peoples who had been subject were using their new nationalism to give expression to their sense of human dignity and corporate identity. The Western churches, it was pointed out, still retained a relatively uncritical attitude towards the traditional structure of international political and economic relations. The so-called "international law" imposed by the West on the rest of the world as a guide for international relations was heavily biased in favour of the Western powers. The report of the Thessalonica Conference, quoted from above, also urges the wealthy countries to reflect on the impact of their actions on others and to be willing to contribute far more to the economic development of poorer nations. There was a growing awareness of the world as an interdependent whole in which no part could plead that its actions did not affect the other parts.

Criticisms such as these convinced the World Council that its social thought was in need of radical re-examination. The New Delhi Assembly recognized this need, but could not supply any answers of itself. The magnitude of the problem led the Assembly to admit the inadequacy of the current ecumenical social ethics as well as its own inability to offer an alternative, more relevant ethic. A long-term search was required if a satisfactory solution was to be found. Out of this concern sprang the proposal for a World Conference on Church and Society.

Preparations for the Conference were made over a period of four years. It was decided that the proceedings should be unofficial in the sense that the Conference would speak to the churches rather than for them. This, it was hoped, would free the deliberations from the inhibiting duty which the Assemblies experienced of having to avoid, as far as possible, statements which could not be supported by nearly all the member churches. The Conference would be free to publish its findings irrespective of their acceptability. If hopes were to be fulfilled and a new basis for social thought was to be found, then the participants must not be hindered in their task by reservations as to how their suggestions would relate to currently accepted modes of thought. It was hoped and expected that their conclusions would be new and prophetic in response to the new challenges arising from the new world situation. There were those who thought, not only in prospect but also in retrospect, that this approach invited irresponsibility. The relatively unqualified opinions of individuals and groups might be published under the auspices of the Conference and be taken by others to have the authority of Assembly Statements. One such critic was Paul Ramsey, whose other criticisms we shall examine later. (70)

Three further requirements were: that the Conference should be composed, as far as possible, of at least as many laymen as clergy, be informed by participants who were experts in various relevant secular fields, and be fully representative of the "third world". At the Conference, which was held in Geneva in July 1966, these requirements were observed. (71) The Conference theme was "Christians in the Technical and Social Revolutions of Our Time". Race was only one of the focal points in this whole field. For at least four reasons, however, it was a preoccupation at Geneva. First, it remained part of the on-going ecumenical concern. Secondly, it was announced that the Rt. Rev. Alpheus Zulu, an Anglican bishop in South Africa, was unable to attend because he had been denied a passport by the South African government. Thirdly, prior to the Conference the International Court of Justice had decided by a single vote, and that on a technicality, to dismiss a six-year suit brought by Ethiopia and Liberia to end South Africa's control of South West Africa. Fourthly, Dr. Martin Luther King was scheduled to preach at an ecumenical service of worship held in the Cathedral of St. Pierre, Geneva, during the Conference, but was prevented from coming by race riots in Chicago. His sermon was filmed and screened at the service. It was also relayed on the European television network and viewed by millions. The seriousness of world racial problems was thus impressed on the minds of the participants and of the public at large.

The procedures and findings at Geneva were, as we shall see, by no means universally applauded. Their impact, however, was enormous. Almost all the departments of the World Council were influenced and began to see their work in the light of the Conference findings. Co-operation with the Roman Catholic Church received a boost when it was realized that the preoccupations of Geneva resembled those underlying Roman Catholic social documents such as Gaudium et Spes. The independent yet common concerns were confirmation of the fact that Christian social thought was indeed being addressed to problems currently experienced by men in the contemporary world.

Some critics felt that the attention paid to those problems was exaggerated. Demosthenes Savramis, for instance, speaks of the "neo-conformity between the church and the spirit of the age". Many theologians, he feels, are attracted by popularized sociology from which they derive jargon-words such as "social", "establishment", "manipulation", "repression", "consumer society", "affluent society" and the most popular and hackneyed of all, "revolution". He is in no doubt as to where this route leads.

> The result is a kind of pop-theology in imitation of the pop-politics and pop-sociology which are such characteristic ingredients of the sub-culture of contemporary youth protest. (72)

We may wonder whether Savramis is as convinced of the newness of the social problems facing the churches as were the organizers of the Geneva Conference. In his observation of the interactions of theology and society, he acknowledges that theology and the church are genuinely trying to understand contemporary man and to help him. At the same time he is afraid of the danger of anthropocentricity, of placing man at the centre of all theological concerns. The Geneva Conference was willing to take that risk in the interests of knowing the world and its problems. Without such knowledge, Christian contributions and solutions could hardly be hoped for. How can a solution be sought when the problem is unknown?

The over-riding concern at Geneva was to provide Christian social thinking with a clear view of the life of mankind in the world. On such a factual, empirical base it was hoped that a relevant social ethic could be constructed. It would be a mistake, however, to imagine that the ideas formulated at Geneva and developed up to the Uppsala Assembly were thoroughly objective and based on value-free "facts". As with all other human attempts the Geneva formulations had no divinely provided clarity of vision free from interpretative assumptions which coloured the final product. Certain influential presuppositions underlay the deliberations of the Conference. Among the most important of these were those concerning man and his environment.

No definite concept of man was articulated either at Geneva or at Uppsala, yet the term "the human" was given the role of a key criterion. Uppsala, for instance, said in its report on World Economic and Social Development:

> The central issue in development is the criteria of the human. We reject a definition of development which makes man the object of the operation of mechanical forces, but view it as a process with potenial for promoting social and economic justice and world community and as an encounter between human beings. (73)

In its equivalent report Geneva stressed that:

> Technology must be made to serve human purposes and not be allowed to overwhelm them.

It continued, however, to imply that a clear understanding of what was intended by the term was hoped for rather than at hand.

> This means that Christian theology must expound and defend the understanding of the human as a criterion for judging economic and social change. (This indeed is the purpose of the concept of "the responsible society", which has played a useful part in Christian social thinking in recent years.)

The direction is indicated in which a clear understanding should be sought

> The Christian understanding of the human derives from the belief that Jesus Christ is the disclosure to us of both true God and true Man. In him we see most clearly what it means to say that man is made in the image of God, that in his dealing with the material world the Christian is called to express the Lordship of Christ, and to do so with a sense of solidarity with all men.

The question of the precise nature of this key criterion, however, is recognized as remaining open. A footnote to the above quotation admits as much.

> In stressing the criterion of the human we are aware that there is no full theological agreement on the meaning of our humanity in Christ. Moreover, in the behavioural sciences the empirical understanding of the person is varied. The two need to be related, and the World Council of Churches could usefully invite a group of theologians and social scientists to study this question. (74)

Bearing in mind the unformed nature of the concept of the human, we take notice of two important factors. The first is the dominant position to which the concept was elevated. The second is the fact that certain presuppositions concerning man appear to enjoy wide acceptance.

One of these is the <u>corporate view</u> of man. "Human solidarity" is a recurrent term in the Geneva reports. It seems to indicate more than was intended in previous references in ecumenical thought to the "brotherhood of man". This brotherhood was often understood to be primarily a collection of individuals who, because of their Christian convictions, had come to see their obligation as "their brother's keeper". The reversal of this order and the new priority of the corporate view of man is well illustrated in the Geneva section on "The Nature and Function of the State in a Revolutionary Age".

> Christians find the idea of person-in-community the integral focus of all questions of freedom, justice, peace and equality. (75)

One wonders why the terms "the human" or simply "person" were not felt to be adequate here. The answer may well lie in the probability that there is operative at this point a strongly corporate view of man. In this view the identity of the individual is determined by his social grouping. It is interesting

39

that a seemingly incompatible statement occurs in the same paragraph.

> Yet as persons they transcend all social, economic and political groupings ...

Here we have what appears to be a counter-balance and a corrective to an extreme corporate emphasis, a view which was strongly represented at Geneva and highly influential in subsequent social thought within the World Council.

A further presupposition concerning man is a marked <u>optimism.</u> Related to the belief that man's social environment largely shapes his individual nature is the idea that social justice alone will issue in world community and universal co-operation and well-being. The establishment of institutions to promote human dignity therefore is elevated to a position in ethics above the changing of human attitudes. The sin of the individual is relegated in importance below the injustice perpetuated in outmoded institutions. The mood of the Conference reflects the underlying optimistic assumption that man had it in his power to shape his life-world as he will. It is not seen as an easy task, but neither is it impossible. By reshaping the structures within which he lives man-in-community and, consequently, each man separately will enjoy a new and higher form of existence.

These ideas are reminiscent of the "social gospel" which was influential in the early years of the Life and Work movement, but three significant differences are apparent. The far stronger optimism of Geneva sees technological man as all but the master of his own fate. Man is the transformer of nature. He has the power to understand it, to master it and to use it according to his own ends. An element of stewardship is acknowledged in accordance with the conviction that nature is God's creation and that in it his purposes are being worked out. The theme of man's stewardship is, however, subordinate to that of man's mastery. Secondly, the primacy of a corporate, "solidaristic" view of mankind is far more established and widely accepted than it was in the day of the 'social gospel'. Thirdly, the notion of man's human environment as being in a state of change is new in its elevation to the status of a datum which is basic to any acceptable analysis of society.

This notion of a <u>dynamic universe</u> becomes essential to any valid approach to an understanding of man. It is a third presupposition of the Geneva Conference. If it is accepted that what man is in community shapes what man is in himself, and also that his social environment is changing, then man is himself in a state of change. Egbert de Vries deals with this third underlying assumption in one of the volumes of background material for the Conference. In his words:

> Men and society change under the impact of forces ...

The optimistic attitude towards this change is evident in his view of the potential in the "forces" which are at work in the world. These forces,

> ... can in turn become tools in the hands of man-himself, to be

used within a framework of rules and regulations or of structures, which man can change.(76)

Yet de Vries makes no attempt to hide his uncertainty as to the nature of 'man-himself' or of the structures of which he speaks. Such open-ended thinking, expressive more of a search than of a body of teaching based on new discoveries, is characteristic of social thought within the World Council at this time. De Vries is not certain as to whether "man-himself" can be identified, or whether he is an entity, even if a changing entity. Clearly a general understanding of "human nature", depending as it usually had previously on the idea of a being who in all essential respects remains the same, has no place in such thinking. Likewise, the rules and structures which shape human life do not follow directly from revelation, nor are they inherent in an ordained natural order. They are to be established by human creativity rather than discovered from some transcendent source. Man, then, is pliable. His mind can be moulded. He can be influenced in many ways, even unconsciously. Yet, almost paradoxically, man has it in his power to shape the ways in which he is to be shaped.

One may well ask whether man has some guide in this heavily responsible task. In terms of what will he seek to shape the structures, which will in turn shape him? Towards what goal will his strivings and shapings aspire? One feels that lurking behind the discussions of man as primarily man-in-community is the powerful conviction, which we noted earlier as a corrective to extreme corporate and deterministic views, that men-in-themselves have the potential, as individuals or groups, to transcend their social and political environment. How else would truly creative thought be possible? How, for instance, would the idea of better relations between people of different races and communities be feasible? How could hopeful ideas of man's capacity to establish a better world be sustained?

A well-developed conception of man was absent, yet social thought at Geneva and Uppsala still operated with optimistic assumptions of man's capacities. De Vries, once again, is typical. For him there is a break between the old world and the new. Modern society is characterized by a continuous flow of processes as symbolized by industry, whereas traditional society is characterized by rhythmic processes as symbolized in agriculture. The characteristics of modernity are ethically neutral, yet they allow for "certain spiritual values" such as "creativity", "opportunity to serve", and "freedom".(77) Man is seen as being capable of making the most of these opportunities, yet his awareness of them does not spring directly from within himself or from his community. They are, for de Vries, values derived from the gospel and from Christian revelation. For an adequate treatment of man, even changing man in a new world, he is forced to resort to norms that were operative in the old world.

As we have seen, the need for a wider theological agreement on "the human" was acknowledged at the Geneva Conference. After the Uppsala Assembly the World Council joined with the Roman Catholic Church in the

Humanum Foundation, and initiated a search for a coneption of man which would be widely acceptable. In this search, as at Geneva, dynamic categories of thought are employed, but emphasis is also laid on the dignity and worth of the human person, a safeguard which underlay the 1965 Vatican Council's <u>Gaudium et Spes</u>. The general thrust of the Humanum Studies is illustrated in the thought of David Jenkins. He acknowledges that man is part of the social and material milieu in which he finds himself. Yet man also has the ability to make decisions about how that milieu <u>should</u> be shaped. His science and technology is bringing about a situation where he is to an increasing extent creating his own environment and thus creating himself. He is, therefore faced all the more by the question: how <u>ought</u> I to organize my world? The general direction in which he looks will be that of the promotion of his humanity. In seeking an answer he finds that the concept of "human" with which he operates changes in sense from descriptive to prescriptive. He finds that empirical facts alone can not say all that there is to be said about the human situation. Something about being human gives men the potential to go beyond themselves.

> Hence it is that men must not be and need not be reduced to a function of, or merely a component part of, their world seen either as material process or as history. They have the potentiality of standing out from, that is of becoming transcendent over all that which might be thought, at the level of scientific observation, to condition and determine them. Men have, therefore, a real opportunity, built into the wider nature of things, to be themselves. (78)

The debate continues between what have been called the "vertical" and the "horizontal" conceptions of man. It has its ramifications in uncertainty concerning the nature of the whole Christian life. Norman Goodall quotes an Orthodox participant in the Uppsala Assembly as asking about the Christian Churches and the World Council:

> Should they move in a vertical direction, aiming mainly in the first place at conversion, rebirth, and fulfilment of man in Christ? Or in the horizontal direction in an activist style, aiming at the curing of the evils of the world, the betterment of the conditions of human life and the creation of a normal order of things on this earth? (79)

We have seen that knowledge of the state of the world, especially the empirical factors influencing man's condition, was central to the purpose of the Geneva Conference. One of the motivating convictions of the Conference was that widespread radical change was a fact of modern life. The term which came to describe all the various kinds of change was <u>revolution</u>. Used in ecumenical discussion at least as early as 1949, (80) it was a key term both in the title and the thinking of the Geneva Conference.

In addition to its use as an umbrella description of all the changes taking place, at least two further senses of "revolution" can be detected. Both are related to human response and action. First, the fact of revolutionary activities of men which take place in the changing world is recognized.

Revolutionary thought and action, the basic rejection of the present world system of power and order and the determination to overthrow it, are more alive in our world than in that of a generation ago. (81)

Secondly, the word assumes a prescriptive function. Christians ought to participate in revolutionary activity. It is a right response to the "Technical and Social Revolutions of our Time".

Such encouragement, however, is found at many levels. At its weakest it is little more than a form of permission to Christians.

> As Christians we are committed to working for the transformation of society ... Today, a significant number of those who are dedicated to the service of Christ and their neighbour assume a more radical or revolutionary position. (82)

This is the approach normally encountered within the World Council. The kind of action which may be involved in this "radical or revolutionary action" covers a broad spectrum. At Uppsala it was emphasized that revolution must not be identified with violence. (83) Revolution by military action may sometimes be necessary, but is never, for the Christian, one option among many. It is always an <u>ultima ratio</u>, to be considered only when all non-violent possibilities have failed.

Encouragement to participate in revolution occurs in a far stronger form. Richard Shaull is representative of those participants in ecumenical discussion who see involvement in revolution as a duty incumbent on Christians and on the churches. Shaull claims that social revolution is a "primary fact" with which we will have to come to terms. It has come about through a process of polarization of races and classes and is the most characteristic fact of contemporary society. This "primary fact", however, contains an "ought". It is interesting to note how Shaull moves from what looks like a descriptive claim to a prescription without introducing any extraneous value reference. If the above claim is correct, he argues,

> it will be on the frontiers of revolution that many of the major issues of humanization and dehumanization will be decided in our modern world; it will be on these frontiers that those most concerned for the well-being and for the future of man will find themselves involved.

It seems that the latter phrase might be changed to "... <u>ought</u> to find themselves involved", without in any way changing the sense. As Shaull continues the imperative note is sounded more strongly.

> If we hope to preserve the most important elements of our cultural, moral and religious heritage and to contribute to the shaping of the future, we cannot remain outside the revolutionary struggle or withdraw from it. (84)

We shall have occasion in a moment to examine the basis on which Shaull argues for revolution simultaneously as a fact and as a value.

There was within the World Council a body of opinion very dubious of the somewhat vague and uncritical attitudes towards revolution that seemed to be gaining ground. A consultation at Zagorsk in 1968 had as its task a theological appraisal of the Geneva Report. The statement of the consultation points out some of the dangers inherent in the use at Geneva of the term "revolution". It is an imprecise term open to many diverse interpretations. When it takes the form of a power struggle revolution tends to "absolutize" and "harden" itself. When attitudes take this form they are as wrong as those, critically dealt with at Geneva, which see any given form of the state as sacral or immutable. Violent revolution breeds violence and the duty of Christians will be to control and minimize that violence. Finally, ambiguity in political ethics in a revolutionary situation can not be eradicated even by means of theological understanding and Christian participation. Specific decisions have to be taken which may have good or evil results. Indeed there is no assurance that a revolution, once carried through, will issue in a more just social order than the one replaced.

> Despite these reservations Zagorsk advised that:
> Christians have a duty to be identified with people as they seek new structures of social justice which meet their human demands to live responsibly. (85)

The reservations led, however, to alternative terminology being sought. We detect above, for instance, an echo of "the responsible society" concept (see page 16). The most influential of the alternatives is "development" which the papal encyclical Polpulorum Progressio describes as "the new name for peace". (86)

For Shaull the fact of revolution in the world is decisive. Zagorsk, on the other hand, finds it necessary to look beyond the facts for "human ends" which must be the aims of any new orders of society. Shaull seems to find all the "values" he requires in the acceptance of revolution as a truth about the world. Zagorsk speaks of the fulfilment of God's promise to renew all things which is present already in Christ, and sees in the light of this promise the possibility both to accept and to criticise the revolutionary trends in the world. (87) Clearly the tendency is towards criteria on which revolutions might be judged. This is a welcome corrective to the approach of Shaull. It is difficult to see how he would, while remaining within his own terms, distinguish between a good and a bad revolution or discern that one revolutionary group is better than another.

The basis for the thinking of Shaull is contextual ethics. He assumes that the most important consideration, possibly the only necessary consideration, in making moral decisions is an adequate knowledge of the facts. He concedes that general principles have played an important role in Christian ethics in the past, but believes that they are not able to deal effectively with "the concreteness of the revolutionary process" or to give sufficient attention to the knowledge of the specialist.

Shaull is strongly influenced by the ethics of Paul Lehmann who seeks to reduce all "ought" statements of "is" statements. A Christian's only guide lies neither in rules nor in general principles, but in the fact of God's action in the world. A Christian is one who is involved in what God is doing in the world, and that is:

> ... setting up and carrying out the conditions for what it takes to keep human life human. (88)

The conclusion of Shaull's argument reveals a naive optimism about man's capacity to gather all the facts in any given problem, to analyse and interpret them correctly and, having done so, to act morally in an automatic fashion.

> When technical insight is set in the context of the humanizing activity of God, it makes sense to affirm that once the full facts are known, the appropriate action will follow. (89)

Shaull is an extreme rather than a typical example of the new direction taken by the World Council in its social thought. There is no doubt, however, that the most influential ethical basis at Geneva and in subsequent discussions was the kind of contextualism described above. Indeed, it seems natural, considering the purpose of World Council thinking first to know the new world as an empirical reality and then to seek an adequate ethic, that contextualism should emerge as an appropriate basis. Fixed and unchanging general principles based on formally correct theolical positions, be they of the Biblically-based or the natural law variety, had been seen to carry no guarantee against arriving at irrelevant or even corrupt conclusions. Such conclusions it was felt were likely to be reached if a grasp was not had of necessary empirical details. The pressing need was to know the facts of the case, in terms of which appropriate action could be planned. Included in this knowledge would be an informed view of the various consequences likely to follow from a proposed course of action. Even when all these facts were known there was no certainty as to whether principles of the kind previously used would be acceptable. One of the central convictions about the world, as we have seen, was that it was in a state of change. If principles were once again to be sought they would have to be dynamic to be applicable. Geneva expresses well the underlying mood.

> For many, the need for the eternal and the absolute seems to have been suppressed by the pressures of life. (90)

The Bible is helpful, it continues, in that it is concerned, not with abstract and timeless structure of thought, society and the physical world, but with a truth that is lived out within the ongoing historical process and is open to the future.

Our task, in this chapter, is not to develop a critique of the social thought of the World Council. Rather are we concerned with surveying some important changes in the direction of that thought. We may note briefly, however, some difficulties that become apparent. First, the distinctiveness of the Christian witness is greatly weakened. This danger was recognized earlier in the Rapid Social Change study.(91) For the World Council, however, it was a risk worth taking. Secondly, Christians and the church, it seems, only react after being aroused by secular events. They do not initiate action in terms of their own convictions. Further, there is the belief that God is at work in the world, but no means are readily available to locate and recognize that divine activity. There is clearly a need for criteria in terms of which some certainty may be had to guard against mistakes concerning "what God is doing in the world". John Bennett's illustration is relevant here.(92) He reminds us that many churchmen saw God at work positively in Hitler. Finally, there is a danger that theology may be employed simply as a justification for social, political or economic decisions and doctrines in the shaping of which theology itself has played no influential role. The Zagorsk Consultation makes the commendable suggestion that the way forward in the ecumenical ethical debate may lie neither in deductive nor inductive methods in themselves. A "method of dialectical interaction" should be sought in which full weight is given to both approaches. The findings of each are channelled into an interdisciplinary dialogue in which moral guidance for action would be found. Conclusions will not be reached easily, but the pitfalls of pure contextualism noted above and the irrelevance of eternally valid general principles would be avoided. In such a scheme there would be a place on the one hand for the empirical findings of the expert work of the social scientist and the other hand for Biblical guidelines and such a helpful concept as 'the responsible society', each side being informed by the other.

Related to the debate over ethical bases is the question of the purpose of Christian social thought. The call at Geneva and afterwards was for <u>specific projects</u> to be outlined rather than for principles to be formulated in the hope that appropriate action on the part of the churches would follow. This call is exemplified in the following quotation:

> ... many church projects suffer from lack of precision and clarity in defining objectives, methods and timetable; too often goals are couched in vague moral terms. Projects should be defined with concrete and achievable (measurable if possible) objectives. These goals need to be specific not only in terms of what is to be accomplished, but also why the specific goals are particularly relevant and suited to the concrete situation ... There is no excuse for lazy and amateurish thinking, such as that which leads to the opening of a college "because country X needs more educated people". This is a abuse of a opportunity and responsibility.(93)

A strongly critical response towards this function of social ethics to produce specific and detailed policies comes from Paul Ramsey. He distinguishes between these "policy - directives" which he says are an abuse, and "decision-oriented or action-oriented social and political analysis" which he sees as the proper task of social ethics. The churches should provide not directives, supported by an "ad hoc theology", but directions which are helpful to Christians as they attempt to act with prudence in the secular sphere. Ramsey does admit that purely general statements are not enough, and that some knowledge of empirical factors in a situation is essential. His aim, however, is to avoid merely providing prejudices and partisan causes with religious sanction. Within such a framework all those who hold alternative views are, by implication, at fault even though they may claim a justification for their position in Christian theology.

The method Ramsey advocates is that which seeks to formulate "middle axioms". These are broad principles for action which are derived from relating general moral principles, such as Christian love, to limited areas of concern, such as racial justice. He regards the Oxford Conference of 1937 as the high point in the search for an ecumenical social ethic of this kind which encourages rationality in judgement. Similar though this criticism is to some of the points we have made concerning ethical thinking within the World Council, and useful though it is as a caution against both pure contextualism and uncontrolled specificity, one wonders whether Ramsey's main difficulty may not stem from an inability to acknowledge the very factors which made the Geneva Conference necessary. One wonders whether the two-realms framework on which he relies so heavily deals adequately with some of the main considerations at Geneva: the secular pluralistic social order as distinct from a unified Christendom; corporate man as distinct from the individual Christian; and a dynamic rather than static world-view. It seems that the suggestion at Zagorsk of a "method of dialectical interaction", although similar to that of Ramsey in that it is also a middle way, is more appropriate to the present requirements of Christian social ethics.

Before turning to the policy and action on race relations which flowed from the changes in direction of World Council social ethics, we may profitably note the effect the changes had on the thought of Daisuke Kitagawa. In his earlier writings the aims and methods which were characteristic of the work of the Secretariat for Racial and Ethnic Relations are dominant.(94) Information is gained through study of racial problems. This information is used for educational purposes, and education is envisaged as taking place primarily within and between churches. The danger to be fought against is the threat which racial divisions pose to the belief of individual Christians, to the community life of the churches, and to the progress of the whole ecumenical movement. It was hoped that education would lead to changed attitudes and that thereby the course of inter-group reconciliation and healthy race relations would be furthered. These were Kitagawa's main aims.

The essay which Kitagawa contributed to the preparatory material for the Geneva Conference reveals marked changes which are a challenge to the policy hitherto pursued by the Secretariat. Education and the dissemination of correct information are no longer seen as constituting a viable method. This method rests on a faulty view of the nature of the problem.

> The problem of racial prejudice cannot be adequately dealt with by exhortation or even by scientific analyses. The problem is not only how to correct and remove a certain kind of misinformation

> about different racial groups. The outlook on man of prejudiced
> people is warped in spite of all the scientific findings in the area
> of biology, cultural anthropology and even moral theology; and
> this outlook defies rational argument.(95)

Kitagawa now sees racial tensions in terms of power struggle rather than in terms of personal and group relationships. He is now critical of the approach taken for so long by the church, which is satisfied with personal friendships between people of different races and with the display of a liberal attitude freed from race prejudice. The problem is located in the structure of society and every effort must be made to change the social pattern itself. Depending on the context, these efforts may be legal or illegal. The law of a land may itself stand in need of change in which case pressure must be applied to this end. The means employed should be non-violent if possible, but circumstances may force a resort to violence.

The focus of Kitagawa's interest has moved from the church towards the world. The function of Christians, however, is still seen as being of crucial importance.

> We need a community of men and women who, under the impact
> of the gospel, have been reunited, who have transcended their
> racial differences to form a reintegrated community, and who
> may be able to act as an integrating force within the still divided
> world.(96)

More clearly than at the Geneva Conference generally, man is viewed by Kitagawa as being able to transcend his environment and, as reconciled himself, to perform a reconciling function. In the exercise of these abilities man's individual decisions are important. Yet the "in-community" theme is not absent, for his individual decisions are seen largely in terms of man choosing between communities. Despite real differences, however, and the retention of much of his previous social philosophy, it is clear that Kitagawa was strongly influenced by the general climate of thought which we have considered in this chapter.

Chapter IV
POLICY AND ACTION - II: CONFRONTATION AND CONFLICT

The culmination, as regards race relations, of the developments we have surveyed was the establishment of a programme within the structure of the World Council whose sole function was to "combat racism". This venture replaced the Secretariat on Racial and Ethnic Relations. Eugene Carson Blake avers that the mandate of the Secretariat was too limited for it to be effective. (97) This dismissal of the work of the Secretariat is somewhat harsh. There can be not doubt that, within its own terms, it did have some success in furthering the cause of improved race relations by keeping the subject in the forefront of the social concern of the churches. In terms of the growing demand for action, however, particularly that which attended and followed the Geneva Conference, Blake's assertion is substantially valid.

Reference was made, at the conclusion of the second chapter, to the relation which pertained between study and action. We saw that the two activities were held to be inextricably intertwined. In fact study in itself was taken to be a kind of action. We also noted throughout that chapter the emphasis on study as a means to solve the problems at hand. To be more precise, study was seen as the means by which principles for action might be formulated. In terms of these principles appropriate action could then be undertaken, but by whom it was not certain. At Geneva the long-felt dissatisfaction with this method was thoroughly articulated. The emphasis swung heavily onto the side of action. The Programme to Combat Racism was to be essentially an action rather than a study programme. The kind of action envisaged followed closely the lines of thought which emerged from the Geneva Conference.

It would be misleading, however, to think of Geneva, crucial though it was, as the <u>sine qua non</u> of the policies which followed. Three examples may be cited in support of this claim. At the beginning of the decade it had been recognized within the Rapid Social Change study that Christian social action was too limited by far in its vision and scope. Churches and missions had yet to see God at work in the social revolution and in the whole process of nation-building. Previous efforts had been made under the influence of the Christendom concept. The aim had been to bring the benefits of Christian civilization to poor countries. Social action of this type had brought upon itself a state of paralysis and had threatened to render itself totally irrelevant.

> There has consequently been a tendency for the Church to restrict itself to those areas of service and action where it can continue to hold to its conception of Christian fellowship and community with the least compromise. Its emphasis on schools, hospitals, and other technical services has been the outcome of this approach. The result of this strategy seems clear: constant withdrawal, leading to the eventual extinction of Christian social action when the technical services of the churches are no longer essential to the state. Such activity may place churches <u>alongside</u> the cultural-social revolution but it does not involve them <u>in</u> it. (98)

Secondly, there is the support which the World Council gave to the Mississippi Delta Project. In 1964 the National Council of the Churches of Christ in the United States requested the support of the World Council in this project. In the Mississippi Delta area racial injustice had been instrumental in bringing about a state of poverty and degradation for many. Relations between racial groups were hostile. It was hoped that the plans for direct relief for the needy, literacy training, the establishment of a cooperative society for black traders and general community development would help in the civil rights struggle, improve race relations and contribute towards the health of the whole society. The World Council voted to provide approximately forty per cent of the cost of the total enterprise and a number of personnel also. The project was still receiving substantial support from the World Council at the end of 1969. The significance of the undertaking for our study is largely symbolic. The churches in the United States were perfectly capable of supporting the project alone. The action of the World Council and its member churches, many of which were in the poor, non-Western nations, symbolized both the interdependence of the modern world and also the truth that those poor nations had much to contribute to Christian life and thought in the rich Western countries. For the first time, financial support was allowed to flow in reverse, from "East" to "West", and the sum was at least three times greater than that later allocated to any single recipient of grants by the Programme to Combat Racism.

Thirdly, the Central Committee, at its 1965 meeting in Enugu, Nigeria, discussed an Ecumenical Programme for Emergency Action in Africa which had been authorized by the Executive Committee the previous year. It called for a sum of ten million dollars over a period of five years to finance a programme of urgently needed nation-building projects and the relief and rehabilitation of refugees, especially the victims of political upheaval throughout the continent. Support would also be given to those imprisoned for their part in the struggle for racial justice. Funds would be made available for their defence and their families would be aided in their absence. Clearly this was to be more than the usual refugee work undertaken by the Division of Inter-Church Aid, Refugee and World Service. In his outline of the programme, Z.K. Matthews said that the aim was to make sure that the church did not take a back seat in the African revolution. (99) The increasing willingness of the World Council to take sides through specific action in political struggles and to participate in revolutionary changes of various kinds is apparent.

The examples cited indicate that the Programme to Combat Racism did have precursors prior to the Geneva Conference. There can be no doubt, however, that the Conference which was a watershed in the social thought of the World Council, was by far the main inspirer of all policy on racial matters after 1966. It supplied the categories of thought and clarified the context in which action should occur. As we have seen, that context was the contemporary revolutions. In its recognition and approval of revolutionary attitudes Geneva noted their significance for racial struggles.

> This revolutionary stance may arise within a nation, a racial group, a class or a generation. (100)

The Conference condemned "ethnocentrism"(101) and noted that the white race dominated the world economically and politically. This domination was seen as preventing the development of authentic human community both within nations and on an international level. We see the concept of "the human" and of "revolutions" operative in the recommendation that:

> Christians should be passionately concerned that this pattern of domination be broken down, in order that a more truly human society may be built.

The close parallel drawn to the point of identification, between social revolutions and God's purposes in history, is nowhere more clearly illustrated than in this report which continues:

> Christian theology has the responsibility to see this situation in historical perspective and to discern the need to destroy this idolatrous structure in order that God's purposes in history may be advanced. (102)

Presupposed here is the contextual principle of knowing "what God is doing in the world".

The method to be used is not that of issuing statements condemning the sin of racial arrogance and oppression. "Costly and bitter engagement" alone will suffice. For Christians to stand aloof from the struggle for radical structural change in society is for them to be disobedient to the call of God in history. (103) The aim of reconciliation is no longer to be pursued in the harmonizing of conflicting groups. Such action alone is mere sentiment. What is required is determination to break down unjust social patterns and to restore the dignity of the oppressed.

> Changes in personal attitudes and reconciliation of individuals are of fundamental importance, but nothing less than structural change can create a pattern of justice in which the dignity and freedom of all will be assured. (104)

The type of society envisaged was not comprised of individuals of various racial backgrounds integrated into one concordant whole. The ultimate unity of the human race was upheld, particularly in the light of the Christian doctrines of creation and redemption, but pluralism was accepted as a necessary pattern. Only by belonging to and by reference to specific ethnic and cultural groups could individuals have a sense of identity. These groups ought not to be exclusive and relations between them, naturally, ought to be equitable and just. Such a "new community" is well described as being "ethnically plural but racially one". (105)

Thus the Geneva Conference created a new mood and pointed firmly in the direction in which World Council policy on racial matters was to move. The Conference itself could not frame that policy. It spoke _to_ the churches-it challenged them and made recommendations for future action. Official policy based on those recommendations could not be made until the Fourth Assembly at Uppsala in 1968.

One of the distinctive characteristics of the <u>Uppsala Assembly</u> was its use of a term later to gain currency in ecumenical discussion, namely "racism". A definition of the term was given. This we quote in full.

> By racism we mean ethnocentric pride in one's own racial group and preference for the distinctive characteristics of that group; belief that these characteristics are fundamentally biological in nature and are thus transmitted to succeeding generations; strong negative feelings towards other groups who do not share these characteristics coupled with the thrust to discriminate against and exclude the outgroup from full participation in the life of the community. (106)

This concept concerns itself with beliefs and attitudes and, in itself, is no substantial advance on the language of Evanston. Like Geneva, however, which spoke of race distinction being absolutized by men and thus becoming a false source of self-identity, the pronouncements of this Assembly must be understood in terms of the new ethical context. The most insidious aspect of racism lies in the fact that it is perpetuated in institutions. The method of dealing with it therefore, must be seen in terms of changing those institutions, local customs, social and national conventions and laws, and the nature of international relationships.

Just as previous statements had pointed out the serious theological significance of such racial attitudes, Uppsala condemned racism on three grounds as "a blatant denial of the Christian Faith". It is a denial of the effectiveness of the reconciling work of Jesus Christ; it denies our common humanity in creation and the belief that all men are made in God's image; and it falsely asserts that our significance is to be found in terms of racial identity rather than in Jesus Christ. Racism was also condemned because of its effect of robbing all human rights of their meaning, because it impedes and distorts development, both diminishing the humanity of white racists and brutalizing those who suffer descrimination, and because it constitutes "an imminent danger to world peace".

Unlike previous World Council thought, Uppsala distinguishes various forms of racism and makes it clear that, while all racism is undesirable, a particular form is especially reprehensible. It is <u>white racism</u> which demands attention and action from the churches. In thus limiting the subject the Assembly was not doing something completely new. A tendency had been gaining ground which on the one hand urged solidarity with the oppressed and on the other emphasized the racial component in the gap between rich and poor nations thus suggesting that the guilt must be laid at the door of the wealthy white races. Geneva spoke of the pattern of white domination. The contribution of Uppsala was to clarify and develop this line of thought. A definition is given, as follows:

> By white racism we mean the conscious or unconscious belief in
> the inherent superiority of persons of European ancestry (particu-
> larly those of Northern European origin), which entitles all white
> peoples to a position of dominance and privilege, coupled with the
> belief in the innate inferiority of all darker peoples especially
> those of African ancestry, which justifies their subordination and
> exploitation. (107)

The passage continues, pointing out that white racism is just one among the many forms of ethnocentrism which issue in tensions and conflict throughout the contemporary world. White racism is singled out, however, because of its special historical significance. Its roots lie in the black slave trade and in the economic and political dominance of white Western nations. The stability of those powerful, highly developed nations, which is essential to international peace and development, is now itself threatened by racism and its effects. The widespread revolt against racism is described as one of the most inflammatory elements of the social revolution now sweeping the earth. The threat posed by racial crises in the powerful countries is to be taken as seriously as the threat of nuclear war.

Certain factors influenced the decisions taken and pronouncements made at Uppsala giving them a force and a cutting edge which distinguishes them from their earlier counterparts. A "black caucus" made its presence strongly felt and consistently challenged the World Council in all its major areas of activity pointing out the pervasiveness of white racism. When the new Central Committee was elected this militant group of black ministers and laymen, mainly from the U.S.A., was well represented. Their influence was now to come from within the heart of the decision-making structure of the World Council.

Secondly, two powerful addresses were delivered on the subject, "White Racism or World Community?" (108) Lord Caradon, British representative at the United Nations, referred to race as: "the dominant problem of our time". He expressed his conviction that, coupled as it is with the world problems of poverty, population and youth, it is the most explosive and dangerous issue which the world must face . Action as opposed to gestures and declarations is demanded. Lord Caradon called for every method of persuasion and pressure to be brought to bear on racism. He limited these methods, however, by excluding violence, and thus affords a good example of the considerable body of thought which agreed with that of Martin Luther King. He also urged that the enthusiasm of the new generation for a international campaign to eliminate racism be mobilized. In such a campaign "positive, militant action" would be used. He looked to the World Council for courageous leadership in such an undertaking. The black American novelist, James Baldwin, speaking passionately from within the black experience and from the perspective of black culture, was able to convey with even more impact than Lord Caradon the tragedy and the urgency of the situation. He spoke of the inadequacy of the morality by which the church claims to live in the face of the problems currently confronting people. He feared for the fate of the coming generation if present trends continued, and he doubted whether the guilty civilizations, which mainly claimed to be Christian, had it in their power to change the trends.

> I tremble when I wonder if there is left in the Christian civilizations (and only these civilizations can answer this question - I cannot) the moral energy, the spiritual daring, to atone, to repent, to be born again.

He argued that Christianity had strayed off course and betrayed its own first principles of responsibility for every living soul by becoming embedded in a powerful institutional form. Clearly if Baldwin were to develop an ecclesiology, he would separate the church from any one particular culture. So critical is he of the church as it is presently constituted that he suggests its destruction to be not only desirable but necessary. Supportive of this is his portrayal of an entirely human Jesus as "a disreputable Hebrew criminal" who began a revolution. As at Geneva the particular work of God in the world is viewed in revolutionary terms. For Baldwin, the process which Jesus started may have to be begun again by people equally disreputable, namely those who are black.

The third influence was that of Martin Luther King whose assassination only three months before the commencement of the Assembly, intensified the feelings of urgency in the struggle for racial justice. As at Geneva he was to have preached, this time at the Opening Service. A resolution was adopted expressing the deep sense of loss felt by the church, thanking God for his prophetic ministry, and commending to the churches his method of non-violence as a means of securing social change. The resolution, recognizing that the question of means had been raised in three of the Assembly sections, requested that studies be promoted on the use of non-violent methods. (109)

Finally, the General Secretary of the World Council from its inauguration, W.A. Visser't Hooft, had retired in 1966. His contribution to World Council thought on race relations, as we have seen, was considerable. His place was taken by Eugene Carson Blake. The significance of this change in leadership was felt not only in the Assembly but throughout the World Council. Dr. Blake had himself been deeply immersed in the civil rights struggle during his term of office as Stated Clerk of the Presbyterian Church in the U.S.A. He had experience-based knowledge of the way in which power operates in society and saw controversy as going hand-in-hand with social effectiveness. He was convinced that the integrity of the ecumenical movement hung at least as much upon what Christians were doing in society as upon the doctrinal agreements they formulated between themselves. His leadership was an inspiration and an encouragement to what we have seen as the general mood in the World Council as regards social ethics in general and racism in particular. (110)

At the Assembly an ad hoc group of some ten participants, led by Daisuke Kitagawa, Rena Karefa-Smart and Baldwin Sjollema, met regularly to work on a background document on racism. It was probably due to this group that the greatest contribution of the Assembly was made. No doubt influenced by their work, the Committee on Church and Society recommended a post-Assembly programme for "The Elimination of Racism". The World Council was urged to "undertake a crash programme to guide the Council and the member churches in the urgent matter of racism". This recommendation was adopted and the new Central Committee was requested to carry out the decision. The result was the Consultation on Racism held in Notting Hill, London, in May 1969.

More than any other meeting it is the <u>Notting Hill Consultation</u> that marks the beginning of the new activist stance of the World Council. The Consultation itself called for a change of priorities without which the churches would ensure their increasing irrelevance and the ineffectiveness of their mission in the world. The churches must purge themselves of their identification with racism and take up the responsibility inherent in their nature and calling. The way to achieve this is clear.

> This requires a new order of priorities. In brief, the move from consultation to implementation <u>is</u> the new priority. (111)

It may seem ironical that calls for action issued in yet another consultation. The nature and purpose of the Notting Hill Consultation, however, ought not to be interpreted in the context of the earlier policies implemented in the work of the Secretariat. Indeed, after fulfilling its responsibility of preparing material for the Geneva Conference in 1966, the Secretariat had waned in significance. That year Tom Okuma, who in 1964 had replaced Kitagawa as head of the Secretariat, vacated the post and no successor was appointed. Perhaps it was recognized then that the old policy and structure had not proved sufficiently effective and could not be expected to cope with the new challenges. At Uppsala it was noted that the Secretariat needed to be strengthened. At Notting Hill it became clear that a structure of a new kind was needed. The objective was purely that of elaborating a programme of action against racism. Although it was itself a consultation, we agree with William H. Crane that it representd a change from the politics of consultation to those of confrontation. (112)

Indeed, the meetings were themselves an occasion for confrontation. Notting Hill is an area which has a history of racial tension and even violence. The meetings were often turbulent, in a way that gatherings sponsored by the World Council had not been before. Confrontation came from political extremists on both sides. The public meeting was disturbed by demonstrators of the right-wing National Front who shouted abuse at the speakers. Towards the end of the Consultation, proceedings were interrupted by a group of Black Power representatives whose leader took the microphone and made known certain demands. These events made a deep impression on participants. It seems to have been felt widely among them that the documents produced and the recommendations conveyed were a weighty contribution to and a significant advance in World Council thought, but that the events in which they had shared had been memorable in an inexpressible way.

The report displays a degree of vehemence not seen before towards the limited type of action undertaken by the Secretariat. Recognition to the reality of racism was not enough. There had been a surfeit of statements, resolutions and documents examining racism, condemning it and calling for programmes to eliminate it. Africans suffering under white racist regimes benefitted in no way from such "action".

> They have with justification come to see resolutions against <u>apartheid</u> as cheap and useless weapons in the struggle against racism... (113)

The crucial need was for "costly, effective action". The objective of the consultation was therefore the provision of guidelines for such action and the recommendation of specific means.

In his address Visser't Hooft reflected on previous World Council policy and its failings as follows:

> a) We have believed too much in persuasion by declarations and not been sufficiently aware of the irrational factors in the situation.
>
> b) We have not given adequate attention to the economic factors making for racial injustice.
>
> c) We have insisted too little on the very considerable sacrifices which have to be made if racial justice is to prevail.

He added a further, ongoing weakness.

> d) We have not yet found common answers to the problem of violence and non-violence as methods of transforming present patterns and present structures. (114)

It is significant that while speaking of its many failings Visser't Hooft continues to think in terms of the old policy. He is of the opinion that one of the main functions of the ecumenical movement in racial crises may be to create "occasions of conversation" in which representatives of the movement would participate and thus bring "a wider perspective" into the situation. This is precisely the policy which had proved ineffective in the work of the Secretariat. It is, in a nutshell, the policy which failed at Cottesloe. Even the title-phrase makes use of the old terminology when it refers to "interracial relations".

It would not be correct to assume that the Consultation did not concern itself with race relations. They were simply no longer a primary consideration. A new order of priorities was required.

> The issues at stake are not so much those which concern better relations between races but rather those which concern the rightful and just distribution of power ... (115)

The key concept at Notting Hill was that of power. Racism as defined at Uppsala was understood not only as a misguided and sinful attitude held by individuals or groups but as a component in the unbalanced and explosive distribution of power. More emphatically even than at Geneva it was stressed that any attempt to harmonize relationships, while leaving social structures unchanged, was doomed to failure. The central problem was missed by such an approach, for it failed to recognize the social origin of human problems. No change of attitude could properly bring freedom from the institutions in which unjust power was embodied. The Statement of the Consultation, following the direction set by Geneva and Uppsala before it, explained the cruciality of power and institutions to a proper understanding of racism.

> It has become clear in the week's study and dialogue that racism is in large part an outgrowth of the struggle for power that afflicts all men. Racist ideologies and propaganda are developed and disseminated as tools in economic, political and military struggles for power. Once developed they have a life of their own, finding a place in the traditions and culture of a people ... (116)

Churches are themselves institutions and, as such, they perpetuate sins of various kinds, often including racism. Their guilt is increased because of their reluctance to examine critically their own structures. As with other institutions they are bound up, willingly or unwillingly, in the ongoing power struggles. They can not claim that their position is neutral. Like other institutions they are ranged on one side or the other in relation to racism. What, then, can the churches do in the battle against racism? What form is their ministry of reconciliation to take? Clearly they must seek to purify their own life and to rectify their own structures. More important, however, is the use they make of the weapons they possess to eradicate racism in society at large.

> ... the Church must be willing to be not only an institution of love, but also an institution of action, making inputs into societies to help effect a new balance of power that renders racism impotent. (117)

This distinction between "love" and "action" is problematic. Clearly, action is not incompatible with love in this case, but equally clearly the two are not identical. What is the nature of this action and why ought the church to involve itself in action that is distinct from love? The answer is given in terms of a conviction which had long been influential in World Council thought and in that of the Life and Work movement before it. In the world, institutionalized as it is, the closest approximation to love possible, is justice. The church must realise this and pursue justice. Indeed, unless it seeks a just distribution of power, the church can not expect its talk of love to be plausible.

What constitutes social justice? Working as it does in a contextualist manner, the Consultation does not attempt to describe a just society. The formulation of an end such as the "Responsible Society" which had been so helpful in previous ecumenical discussion was not within the stated purpose of the Consultation. Instead, it offered some guidelines for action. Even these are by no means firm and clear. The reason for this is, as John Vincent points out, that the World Council is only at the beginning of a debate and is about to start experimental action. (118) It is determined to get down to the specific details of action, but at this stage can only pin-point areas in which the church must act. One of the guidelines is the right of people to self-determination. The objective of the key issue of re-distribution of political, social and economic power is:

> ... so that all peoples can participate responsibly in the decisions by which their destinies are determined. (119)

Another guideline is the picture of society as pluralistic. In the debate between integration and pluralism, as the most just models for relations between groups, it was noted that a general pattern could be observed. When a minority group is in power, it wants segregation of others. When a majority group is in power it wants the others to integrate with it. The determining factors seem to be on the one hand, the fear of being dominated and, on the other, the confidence of being able to dominate. In its attempt to formulate a guiding concept for right relations between groups the Consultation found that it faced a difficulty. Certainly legitimate pluralism offers a possibility of an "increase of justice". Given freedom within their own racial and cultural groups people are far better able to pursue their own ways towards self-fulfilment and to use their share of power to shape their community towards that end. This is in keeping with a third guideline, that of identity. Human identity always has its concrete expression and the notion of belonging to a racial group clarifies and enriches our sense of identity. Danger arises, however, when membership in any particular group becomes a denial rather than an expression of the common humanity shared by all mankind. At Notting Hill the debate was left unsettled between the search for particular identity and the universalism of an inter-dependent world, between pluralism and integration. In the case of the countries of Southern Africa dominated by white racism, however, justice was seen to lie in the establishment of "open pluralistic societies".

A further issue on which the Consultation was called to decide was that of reparations. The issue was posed in a forceful manner by the Black Power group which "invaded" the meetings and demanded that the churches compensate black people for past ill-treatment and for the present imbalance of economic power. Without being able to give proper consideration to the subject, the Consultation decided in favour of the demand. The World Council and its member churches were urged to support the principle of "reparations" to exploited peoples and countries. The Central Committee meeting which followed in August, however, reversed this decision. The concept of "reparations" it said was inadequate because it rested largely on the apportionment of guilt for the past and the idea that this could be atoned for simply by financial payment.

The "reparations" question was part of a wider issue. One of the major methods of action approved at Notting Hill lay in the sphere of economic power. The previous year the findings of the Beirut Conference of the joint Vatican and World Council Committee on Society, Development and Peace had shown in detail the clear racial bias in the international distribtuion and ownership of the developed resources of the world. (120) International finance which thus perpetuates racism and, in particular reinforces racist regimes, ought to be re-organized. The method suggested to the churches and to the World Council is that of reviewing their own finances, making known their own assets and ensuring that they were not guilty themselves of participating in and contributing to the imbalance. They should withdraw any investments they might have in countries such as South Africa where there is a blatantly racist element in the national economy. These initiatives should be extended onto an international scale by using the Commission of the Churches on International Affairs as a co-ordinating body. That Commission should then increase pressure upon United Nations organizations and in this way ensure that member governments are faced with the racist elements in their policies. More use should be made of church finances in the support of community development projects among oppressed peoples.

The final point of the Consultation statement gives rise to the question of <u>violent means</u> which, as indicated earlier, was left undecided. It was recommended:

> that all else failing, the Church and churches support resistance movements, including revolutions, which are aimed at the elimination of political or economic tyrany which makes racism possible. (121)

The link between the churches and organizations employing violent means to effect change was to become the most widely publicised and most highly controversial aspect of World Council social policy. Three points must be emphasized on this point. First, the nature of the support to be given is not stipulated. Not all kinds of support are as open to condemnation as, let us say, the provision of arms and ammunition. Secondly, a resort to this measure would only be made in the most extreme cases. It must always be an <u>ultima ratio</u>. Thirdly, as was recognized at Uppsala, the very "law and order" against which such movements militate may itself be an insidious form of violence.

On August 21st 1969, in its meetings at Canterbury, the Central Committee adopted an Ecumenical Programme to Combat Racism (122), which flowed from the recommendations of the Notting Hill Consultation. In its rationale for the Programme the World Council noted the challenge posed by the "pervasiveness, persistence and viciousness" of racism to which many Christians had risen. Many, however, had been immobilized by a sense of the impotence of the churches. It was recognized that, even as they battled against racism, some churches had benefitted from and some had suffered under racially exploitive economic systems. In the face of the deteriorating situation an "ecumenical act of solidarity" was needed. The World Council therefore called upon the churches,

> ... to move beyond charity, grants and traditional programming to relevant and sacrificial action leading to new relationships of dignity and justice among all men and to become agents for the radical reconstruction of society.

Illuminated by the insights which emerged at Geneva, which were expanded at Uppsala and were crystallized at Notting Hill, the justice to be sought was seen in terms of political and economic change. The venture would be instrinsically moral and its effect would be reinforced because of its ecumenical origin.

> There can be no justice in our world without a transfer of economic resources to undergird the redistribution of political power and to make cultural self-determination meaningful. In this transfer of resources a corporate act by the ecumenical fellowship of churches can provide a significant moral lead.(123)

The outline of the five-year programme suggests action which appears to be not essentially different from that previously attempted by the Secretariat. It urges study of many of the problems which had concerned the Secretariat. The difference lies in the general intention of the programme. Its aim is not less than a radical restructuring of racist societies.

The Programme to Combat Racism was to involve the whole World Council. Far from becoming one among the many concerns of one of the Departments, it required the co-ordinated action of all the Departments and Divisions. At least until the restructuring of the World Council, which was envisaged for 1972, it was to be the direct responsibility of the General Secretariat.

A request was made for an annual administrative budget of $ 150,000. In addition to this a Special Fund was to be established. The total sum aimed at by this fund was $ 500,000. Of this it was hoped that the member churches would contribute $ 300,000. The remainder was to come from the general reserve of the World Council, from the Division of Inter-Church Aid, Refugee and World Service and from the Division of World Mission and Evangelism. Before it was adopted, this proposal for the transfer of World Council funds was hotly debated in the Central Committee.(124)

The financial provisions are followed by concluding remarks which place these practical measures in their theological context. The significance of the P.C.R. is shown to be ultimately spiritual.

> Our struggle is not against flesh and blood, It is against the principalities, against the deeply entrenched demonic forces of racial prejudice and hatred that we must battle. Ours is a task of exorcism. The demons operate through our social, economic and political structures. But the root of the problem is as deep as human sin, and only God's love and man's dedicated response can eradicate it.
>
> The World Council's programme is but part of that response. It is God's love and not the hatred of man that must ultimately triumph. By God's love, by the power of His Spirit, some day, soon, we shall overcome.(125)

CONCLUSION

The Programme to Combat Racism was established with astonishing speed. The first proposal for such a programme was made at the Fourth Assembly in July 1968. The Notting Hill Consultation which outlined and recommended a programme was held in May 1969. In August of that year the Central Committee adopted the P.C.R. and granted it a five-year mandate. The Programme's staff and its International Advisory Committee were appointed in February 1970. They met in May and, acting on their recommendations in September, the Executive Committee of the World Council made the first allocation of $ 200,000 from the Special Fund. In little over two years progress had been made from the original proposal to the first specific action. By contrast the establishment of the Secretariat on Racial and Ethnic Relations which we examined in Chapter II was extremely slow. What reasons can now be offered for the contrasting speed with which the P.C.R. was set in motion?

First, the membership of the World Council itself had changed. At the Second Assembly, where the proposal for the Secretariat was adopted 40 of the 160 member churches were from the third world. At Uppsala their number had increased to 103 out of 253. Of the 41 African churches, the majority were from independent countries. The sense of urgency which surrounded the problem of racism increased accordingly. No longer was racism a problem which the World Council, with however much concern, could view from the outside as a mainly Western body.

Secondly, by the time of the Fourth Assembly there was confidence as regards the durability of the World Council. It had established itself as an important and lasting presence in the life of the church in the world. It was far more certain than before of the kind of action which it could undertake and the breadth of vision it could realistically entertain.

Thirdly, as regards the method of social ethics, there was a consensus which was sufficiently secure to allow for the adoption of the P.C.R. There was a widespread mood of impatience with methods which encouraged study in order to derive general principles from the findings. Racism as an evil fact of the contemporary world must be confronted by the united action of the churches. The P.C.R. was to be essentially an action rather than a study programme.

Fourthly, there was clarity as to the target of the proposed action. The Secretariat had operated with the difficult objective of analysing racial discrimination as a problem for the church in all societies. It struggled with issues of many different kinds. It concerned itself with pastoral and ecclesiastical problems such as those of inter-racial marriage and racial churches as well as with racism in society at large. The P.C.R. at once widened its scope and limited the focus of its immediate concern. It looked not primarily at the churches, but at the whole of secular society on their behalf. The fight against racism was to be set within the context of the struggle for world community. The focus of its work, however, was to be "white racism". As the most virulent form of racism in recent history and in the contemporary world, this was the form which it specifically chose to combat.

It is a temptation in thus contrasting the P.C.R. and the Secretariat to dismiss the Secretariat as a total failure and to uphold the P.C.R. as a wholly new and far more relevant venture. This is to over-simplify to the point of error. Both may be judged as valid responses to changing sets of circumstances. One of the greatest disadvantages of the Secretariat, however, was that so many years were allowed to elapse between its conception and its establishment that the circumstances to which it was to relate had changed considerably. As we have seen, a new kind of response was being called for at the very time that the Secretariat began its work. It would also be a mistake to see the P.C.R. as a completely new departure bearing no relation to any previous activity of the World Council. In an important way the Secretariat was its predecessor and pioneer. The P.C.R. was informed by a wealth of previous experiences, including failures. This was an advantage which the Secretariat did not have. The bearing of this factor on the comparative speeds of establishment of the two structures is indicated by Paul Abrecht.

> ... the speed with which the P.C.R. was established in comparison with the previous rather deliberate preparation for (the Secretariat) can be explained by the fact that the P.C.R. benefitted from the early struggles of (the Secretariat) to define a viable programme. (126)

As mentioned above, a consensus was achieved within the World Council on the method of social ethics. It would be misleading to suggest that this was true in all or even most areas of social concern. The claim can be made, however, in the case of racism. It does not seem that the P.C.R. sprang from a conscious dismissal of the "ethic of ends" approach. The urge towards action was the dominant motive and it was this which made the consensus possible. The evil of racism was all too recognisable in the world. The target, white racism, had been pinpointed. Time was not to be lost in attempting to find a suitable ethical system before action was taken. Nor need the policies decided upon be a unified whole in terms of their relation to such a system. The approach must be to select certain priority situations and to respond to them with "multiple strategies". The action undertaken must fit the various situations and was therefore likely to be as varied as the situations themselves. The only unifying requirement was that action should be in accordance with the general purposes of the World Council. In the ethical debate, such contextualism as this falls on the side of the "ethic of inspiration". Starting as it does however, from the concrete situation and making the demands of that situation the main criteria for action, it is most certainly beyond the terms of reference of the earlier debate between an "ethic of ends" and an "ethic of inspiration". It is an inductive not a deductive approach.

There was general agreement within the World Council that it was justified in launching such a specific programme for action. We noted in chapter III the disagreement of Paul Ramsey on the point of the churches speaking specifically. The dividing line here seems to be the degree of seriousness with which one views a moral problem situation. Ramsey agrees,

> ... that at some point, perhaps at the gateway to Auschwitz, the Christian should speak very specifically against the outrageous crimes of his government. (127)

He attempts an answer by pointing out that this is an exceptional case. The vast majority of opinions within the World Council were that racism was also an exception and, as such, called for the specific measures of the P.C.R.

Despite the consensus which we have noted, vigorous attacks were made on the World Council from outside and strong criticisms were made from inside its membership once the P.C.R. was implemented and grants from the Special Fund were allocated. To evaluate the work of the Programme and the criticisms of it is, unfortunately, beyond the scope of this book, but two final comments may be made.

It was feared by some that the controversial nature of the P.C.R. would threaten ecumenical fellowship and result in withdrawals of membership from the World Council. Elisabeth Adler has replied to this. (128) She points out that towards the end of the first five-year mandate of the P.C.R. no church had withdrawn from the World Council as a result of the Programme. The effect of the P.C.R. on ecumenical fellowship is, she admits, more difficult to judge. She is correct in claiming that the existence of the P.C.R. has provided an opportunity for deeper reflection not only on the meaning of membership but also on its actual practice. This leads to the question of the educational significance of the P.C.R.

There can be no doubt that the P.C.R. has given rise to lively discussion in which many have come to see racial and other social issues far more clearly than before. This is a commendable effect, but is it true education in terms of which ecumenical understanding and fellowship can be deepened? A gulf has opened between two groups who are equally convinced of the seriousness of racism. There are those who stress the priestly function of the church and favour a ministry of liberating reconciliation. There are others who stress the prophetic function of the church and favour a ministry of liberating conflict. How is this gulf to be bridged? Awareness of the issues is not enough by itself. A new understanding must be gained of the positive convictions which motivate the action of the churches. Only in the light of such an understanding can the worth of each side of the gulf be seen and each approach be accorded its rightful place.

For the moment World Council action is <u>against</u> racism. The need is for a clarification of the positive goals which the P.C.R. seeks. What is the World Council action <u>for</u>? Where are those positive goals to be sought, in terms of which the <u>work</u> of the P.C.R. may be evaluated? Perhaps the direction is indicated in the prescription of the Canterbury Central Committee meeting.

> The fight against Racism in all its forms must be set within the context of the struggle for World Community, including World Development. (129)

It must be asked what sort of <u>community</u> is to be striven for and what are the nature and purpose of <u>development</u>. These questions can best be answered in terms of a new and deeper understanding of the realities and the potentialities of what it is to be <u>human</u>.

APPENDIX

Outline of a Five-Year Programme of the World Council of Churches.

Clearly a determined attack on Racism must come as a commitment of the W.C.C. and its divisions and departments and will involve:

1. Teams of inquiry focusing on selected areas in Latin America, North America, Asia, Australasia and the Pacific, Europe, Southern Africa, etc. to express ecumenical concern and to assist in formulating guidelines for ecumenical understanding and action;

2. Consultation on selected issues which obstruct common action in achieving racial justice e.g. the problem of sharing economic and political power, including the demand for "reparations" which has been made in a number of quarters, and other proposals for overcoming the economic burden of historic and comtemporary Racism; the meaning of racial identity; anti-semitism; intermarriage;

3. Providing more opportunity for confrontation between those holding different positions on the meaning of racial justice and those advocating different methods for attaining it;

4. Examination of all the means available for promoting political actions towards the bringing about of racial justice, including economic sanctions, both on the part of the member churches and of governments;

5. Assisting the member churches in developing strategies for combatting racial injustice;

6. Examination of the ways in which the churches can stand for the rights of the victims of Racism and meet their needs;

7. Examination of the programmes, budgets and structures of the World Council of Churches with a view to increasing support of efforts for racial justice;

8. Collection and cirulation of the best analyses on racism - including theological analyses - and other data helpful to the churches for the information and education of their members;

9. Encouraging member churches and national and regional Councils of Churches to make the problem of Racism within their own area a priority concern in their programmes.

Central Committee Minutes, 1969, pp. 274 - 275.

NOTES

1. Ed. N. Goodall, The Uppsala Report 1968 Official Report of the Fourth Assembly of the World Council of Churches (Geneva, 1968), p. 466.
2. The Uppsala Report, pp. 480 - 481.
3. L. Pope, The Kingdom Beyond Caste (New York, 1957), p. 30.
4. W. A. Visser 't Hooft, The Ecumenical Movement and the Racial Problem (Paris, 1954), pp. 8 - 9.
5. W. A. Visser 't Hooft, The Ecumenical Movement and the Racial Problem, pp. 34 - 35.
6. D. Kitagawa, Race Relations and Christian Mission (New York, 1964), pp. 24 - 25.
7. Ed. W. A. Visser 't Hooft, The First Assembly of the World Council of Churches The Official Report (London, 1949), p. 56.
8. Amsterdam Report, p. 81.
9. W. A. Visser 't Hooft, Christianity, Race and South African People (New York, 1952).
10. K. G. Grubb, Crypts of Power (London, 1971), pp. 150 - 151.
11. The Christian Hope and the Task of the Churches (New York, 1954), Section on "Intergroup Relations", p. 1.
12. J. H. Oldham, Christianity and the Race Problem (London, 1924), p. 17.
13. J. H. Oldham, Christianity and the Race Problem, p. 22.
14. J. H. Oldham, Christianity and the Race Problem, p. 218.
15. J. H. Oldham, Christianity and the Race Problem, p. 8.
16. W. A. Visser 't Hooft, The Ecumenical Movement and the Racial Problem (Paris, 1954), p. 67.
17. H. D. Wendland, "The Relevance of Eschatology for Social Ethics", The Ecumenical Review, V, 1, (1953), 364.
18. The Amsterdam Report, p. 77.
19. The Christian Hope and the Task of the Churches, Intergroup Relations, pp. 21 - 23.
20. E. Duff, The Social Thought of the World Council of Churches (London, 1956), pp. 93 ff.
21. The Evanston Report The Second Assembly of the World Council of Churches 1954 (London, 1955), p. 159.
22. The Evanston Report, pp. 156 - 157.
23. Ibid., p. 153.
24. Ibid., p. 155.

25. Ibid., p. 158.
26. A. J. van der Bent, The Utopia of World Community (London, 1973), p. 51.
27. World Council of Churches, Minutes and Reports of the Tenth Meeting of the Central Committee, Yale Divinity School, U.S.A., 1957, pp. 28 - 29.
28. Dr. Oscar Lee of the National Council of the Churches of Christ of the U.S.A. recommended such an appointment within the W.C.C. Staff following visits which he made to Africa and Asia in 1956. Secretaries of the various national Christian councils had expressed to him their desire for the help of a W.C.C. consultant.
29. World Council of Churches, Minutes and Reports of the Eleventh Meeting of the Central Committee, Denmark, 1958, p. 104.
30. World Council of Churches, Minutes and Reports of the Twelfth Meeting of the Central Committee, Rhodes, Greece, 1959, p. 52. The expected cost was estimated at $ 12,500 p.a. In the proposed general budget for the period following the Third Assembly adopted by the Central Committee in 1960, the amount was increased to $ 14,000.
31. "Proposals to the Third Assembly for the Secretariat on Racial and Ethnic Relations", W.C.C. Division of Studies, (mimeograph, 1961), pp. 5, 20.
32. Ibid., p. 16.
33. The New Delhi Report The Third Assembly of the World Council of Churches (London, 1962), p. 187.
34. The New Delhi Report, pp. 182 - 185.
35. The phrasing of this point is unclear. The suggestion, presumably, is in keeping with the general trend of ecumenical thought at the time. In that case, what is intended is not a plea for churches or local congregations to be organized on a racial or ethnic basis. Rather, it is an affirmation that the unity within the church transcends all other allegiances.
36. The New Delhi Report, p. 187.
37. "Proposals to the Third Assembly for the Secretariat on Racial and Ethnic Relations", W.C.C. Division of Studies (mimeograph, 1961), p. 16.
38. The New Delhi Report, p. 81.
39. An African Township near Johannesburg where, in March 1960 between sixty and seventy black protesters were shot dead by police.
40. The government policy of compulsory segregation on a racial basis.
41. Quoted in Lesley Cawood, The Churches and Race Relations in South Africa (Johannesburg, 1964), p. 131.
42. Mission in South Africa (Geneva, 1961), pp. 25, 27.
43. Cottesloe Consultation The Report of the Consultation among South African Member Churches of the World Council of Churches (Johannesburg, 1960), p. 74.

44. We noted the influence of this approach in our discussion on the debate between two ethical methods at Amsterdam and Evanston, pp. 18 - 19.
45. Cottesloe Consultation, p. 74.
46. Cottesloe Consultation, p. 75.
47. Cottesloe Consultation, p. 80.
48. E. Strassberger, "Ecumenism in South Africa 1936 - 1960 with Special Reference to the Mission of the Church", (University of Stellenbosch ThD, 1971), p. 377.
49. Roger Lloyd, The Church of England 1900 - 1965 (London, 1966), p. 513.
50. Quoted in W. A. Visser 't Hooft, Memoirs (London, 1973), p. 282.
51. World Council of Churches, Minutes and Reports of the Seventeenth Meeting of the Central Committee, Rochester, New York, U.S.A., 1963, p. 141.
52. Central Committee, 1963, p. 142.
53. The established operations of the Division of Inter-Church Aid, Refugee and World Service may be cited as evidence of the fact that such action by the W.C.C. was by no means new. Indeed the W.C.C. had a proud history of response to human need. The new element indicated above is the Christian response to a specific problem situation in which human need is directly and inextricably bound up with the internal racial policies of a country.
54. Mindolo had repercussions in South Africa which came to a head in a libel trial in August 1967. A. D. Pont, who had accused Prof. A.S. Geyser and the Rev. C. F. Beyers Naude (all of the Dutch Reformed Churches) of treason because of their connection with the W.C.C. and their participation at Mindolo, was ordered to pay costs plus the highest amount to date for damages awarded in a trial of its kind in that country. Summary of Judgement, Johannesburg, 1967.
55. D. A. Etheredge, "Changing Prevailing Racial Patterns through Economic Action", Race Relations in Ecumenical Perspective, 5, (1964), 33.
56. Z. K. Matthews, "The Road from Non-Violence to Violence", Race Relations in Ecumenical Perspective, 5, (1964), 17.
57. Christians and Race Relations in Southern Africa Report on an Ecumenical Consultation on Christian Practice and Desirable Action in Social Change and Race Relations in Southern Africa (Geneva, 1964), p. 15.
58. Christians and Race Relations in Southern Africa, pp. 19 - 20.
59. Christians and Race Relations in Southern Africa, p. 14.
60. D. Kitagawa, "The World Council of Churches and the Race Problem: an Abstract", (Geneva, File of the Secretariat on Racial and Ethnic Relations, undated mimeograph):

61. "Ethnic Tensions in an Emerging Nation - the Case of Ceylon", <u>Race Relations in Ecumenical Perspective</u>, 3 (1962).
62. D. Kitagawa, "The World Council of Churches and the Race Problem: an Abstract", Part II, Functions of the Race Relations Consultant, pp. 2 - 3.
63. D. Kitagawa, "All in Each Place: Racial and Cultural Issues", <u>The Ecumenical Review</u>, XV, 1 (1962), pp. 43 - 56.
64. <u>The New Delhi Report</u>, p. 186.
65. D. Kitagawa, <u>The Pastor and the Race Issue</u> (New York, 1965), p. 105.
66. <u>Central Committee Minutes</u>, 1959, p. 41.
67. Quoted in (ed.) H. E. Fey, <u>The Ecumenical Advance - A History of the Ecumenical Movement</u>, Volume 2, (London, 1970), p. 248.
68. It is of interest that in the few years immediately prior to the integration of the two bodies the W. C. C., in its social thrust, had to co-operate very closely with the I. M. C. In many cases in the regions chosen for study the I. M. C. was the only contact available to the W. C. C. (Pointed out by Dr. Norman Goodall in conversation, 1st April 1974)
69. Quoted in ed. H. E. Fey, <u>The Ecumenical Advance</u>, pp. 249 - 250.
70. Paul Ramsey: <u>Who Speaks for the Church?</u> (Edinburgh, 1969), p. 140.
71. <u>World Conference on Church and Society</u> Official Report (Geneva, 1967), p. 10. Of the 338 participants officially nominated by the churches, 180 were laymen and 158 were theologians. Among the laymen were 50 political leaders and civil servants, 19 businessmen and industrialists, 28 economists, 9 workers or trade union leaders, 20 social scientists and 8 natural scientists. Participants from the Western countries totalled 146, while 147 came from non-Western countries and 45 from Eastern Europe including the U.S.S.R.
72. D. Savramis, "Theology and Society: Ten Hypotheses", ed. R. H. Preston, <u>Technology and Social Justice</u> (London, 1971), p. 401.
73. <u>The Uppsala Report</u>, p. 49.
74. <u>The Geneva Report</u>, pp. 52 - 53. This point is also made in the "Conclusions and Recommendations", p. 90.
75. <u>The Geneva Report</u>, p. 104.
76. E. de Vries, "From Tradition to Modernity", ed. E. de Vries, <u>Man in Community</u>, (New York, 1966), p. 28.
77. E. de Vries, <u>Man in Community</u>, p. 35.
78. David Jenkins, "The Concept of the Human", in ed. R. H. Preston, <u>Technology and Social Change</u>, p. 221.
79. Norman Goodall, <u>Ecumenical Progress</u> (London, 1972), pp. 13 - 14.

80. Paul Abrecht quotes from a statement of the East Asia Christian Conference held in Bangkok, 1949. "The struggle for, and the attainment of, political freedom has awakened the hitherto submerged peoples of East Asia to a new sense of dignity and historical mission. Those are basic elements in the revolutionary ferment which are at work in the contemporary revolts and power-conflicts in Asia". ed. H.Fey, The Ecumenical Advance, p. 247.
81. The Geneva Report, p. 199.
82. The Geneva Report, p. 49.
83. The Uppsala Report, p. 48.
84. Richard Shaull, "Revolutionary Change in Theological Perspective", ed. John C.Bennett, Christian Social Ethics in a Changing World (New York, 1966), p. 25.
85. "Statement of the Zagorsk Consultation", Study Encounter, 4 (1968), 76.
86. Populorum Progressio - papal encyclical (London, 1967), p. 35.
87. Zagorsk Statement, op. cit., p. 76.
88. Paul L.Lehmann, Ethics in a Christian Context (London, 1963), p. 124.
89. Ed. J.C.Bennett, Christian Social Ethics in a Changing World, p. 43.
90. The Geneva Report, p. 199.
91. Paul Abrecht, The Churches and Rapid Social Change (London, 1961), p. 205.
92. John C.Bennett, "Issues for Ecumenical Debate", ed. J.C.Bennett, Christian Social Ethics in a Changing World, p. 376.
93. Richard Dickinson, Line and Plummet (Geneva, 1968), p. 85.
94. See for example: Race Relations and Christian Mission (New York, 1964);
    The Pastor and the Race Issue (New York, 1965);
    "Theological and Non-Theological Factors in Race Relations", The Ecumenical Review, XIII, 1961, pp. 335 - 341.
95. D.Kitagawa, " 'Racial' Man in the Modern World", ed. E.de Vries, Man in Community, p. 147.
96. D.Kitagawa, Man in Community, p. 144.
97. J.J.Vincent, The Race Race (London, 1970), p.x.
98. Paul Abrecht, The Churches and Rapid Social Change (London, 1961) p. 206.
99. World Council of Churches, Minutes and Reports of the Eighteenth Meeting of the Central Committee, Enugu, Nigeria, 1965, p. 17.
100. The Geneva Report, p. 199.
101. The Geneva Report, p. 161. Although this seems to be a new term in World Council discussion, no explanation is offered. It was probably assumed to be self-explanatory. Its meaning is fully expressed in the definition of racism given at the Fourth Assembly.
102. The Geneva Report, p. 204.

103. The Geneva Report, p. 205.
104. The Geneva Report, p. 204.
105. The Geneva Report, p. 206.
106. The Uppsala Report, p. 241. There is a marked similarity between this definition and that issued by UNESCO in 1967. "Racism, namely anti-social beliefs and acts which are based on the fallacy that discriminatory inter-group relations are justifiable on biological grounds ... Racism falsely claims that there is a scientific basis for arranging groups hierarchically in terms of psychological and cultural characteristics that are immutable and innate. In this way it seeks to make existing differences appear inviolable as a means of permanently maintaining current relations between groups." World Council of Churches, Minutes and Reports of the Twenty-Third Meeting of the Central Committee, Canterbury, Great Britain, 1969, p. 270.
107. The Uppsala Report, p. 241.
108. ed. A. H. van den Heuvel, Unity of Mankind: Speeches from the Fourth Assembly of the World Council of Churches, (Geneva, 1969), pp. 50 - 63. Also The Ecumenical Review, XX, 4 (1968), 325 - 463.
109. The Uppsala Report, p. 270.
110. "Blake, the Rev. D. Eugene Carson", World Council of Churches Communication (mimeograph, Geneva, 1971), p. 2.
In correspondence with the writer the Rev. David Gill of the Department on Church and Society recalled how in a staff discussion he had warned that the Notting Hill consultation was likely to involve the World Council in a storm of controversy. D. Blake responded thus: "You may be right, but I am not prepared to keep the World Council of Churches going if it is at the expense of what the World Council of Churches should be standing for."
111. Report on the World Council of Churches Sponsored Consultation on Racism held in Notting Hill, London, May 19 - 24, 1969; (Preparatory Document No. 11 for Central Committee Meeting, Canterbury, England, 1969, mimeograph). Section IV, p. 21.
112. William H. Crane: "From the Politics of Consultation to those of Confrontation," Study Encounter, 5 (1969), pp. 131 - 137.
113. The Notting Hill Report, p. 16.
114. W. A. Visser 't Hooft, "Reflections on World Council of Churches' Action Concerning Interracial Relations"; Address to the Notting Hill Consultation, paper number 6/E (mimeograph, 1969), p. 4.
115. The Notting Hill Report, p. 16.
116. The Notting Hill Report, p. 1.
117. The Notting Hill Report, p. 1.
118. J. J. Vincent, The Race Race p. 49.
119. The Notting Hill Report, p. 16.

120. World Development: The Challenge to the Churches, Official Report of the Conference on World Co-operation for Development, Beirut, 1968 (Geneva, 1968), p. 9. The report states that about 80 per cent of the world's resources are at the disposal of only 20 per cent of the world community, living mainly around the North Atlantic and therefore predominantly white. This gap between rich and poor is increasing.
121. The Notting Hill Report, p. 2.
122. For the outline of the programme, see Appendix.
123. World Council of Churches, Minutes and Reports of the Twenty-Third Meeting of the Central Committee, Canterbury, Great Britain, p. 273.
124. Dr. E.A. Payne opposed the use of reserve funds. He believed that the policy was not only financially questionable, but also morally wrong. Central Committee Minutes, 1969, p. 39.
125. Central Committee Minutes, 1969, p. 277.
126. Paul Abrecht in correspondence with the writer.
127. Paul Ramsey, Who Speaks for the Church? p. 47.
128. Elisabeth Adler, A Small Beginning (Geneva, 1974), pp. 67 - 68.
129. World Council of Churches, Minutes and Reports of the Twenty-Third Meeting of the Central Committee, Canterbury, Great Britain, 1969, p. 272.

BIBLIOGRAPHY

I. Official Minutes and Reports, and Background Material for Meetings

Cottesloe Consultation. The Report of the Consultation among South African Member Churches of the World Council of Churches. Johannesburg: 1960.

Christians and Race Relations in Southern Africa. Report on an Ecumenical Consultation on Christian Practice and Desirable Action in Social Change and Race Relations in Southern Africa. Geneva: W.C.C., 1964.

Goodall, N.(ed.) The Uppsala Report 1968. Official Report of the Fourth Assembly of the World Council of Churches, Uppsala July 4 - 20, 1968. Geneva: W.C.C., 1968.

Mission in South Africa, April - December 1960. Geneva: W.C.C., 1961.

"Proposals to the Third Assembly of the World Council of Churches." W.C.C. Division of Studies. 1961 (Mimeographed.)

"Report on the World Council of Churches Sponsored Consultation on Racism held in Notting Hill, London, May 19 - 24, 1969." Preparatory Document number 11 for Central Committee Meeting, Canterbury, England, 1969. (Mimeographed).

The Christian Hope and the Task of the Church. Six Ecumenical Surveys and the Report of the Assembly prepared by the Advisory Commission on the Main Theme 1954. New York: Harper and Brothers, 1954.

Visser't Hooft, W.A. (ed.) The Evanston Report. The Second Assembly of the World Council of Churches 1954. London: S.C.M., 1955.
The First Assembly of the World Council of Churches. The Official Report. London: S.C.M., 1949.
The New Delhi Report. The Third Assembly of the World Council of Churches 1961. London: S.C.M., 1962.

World Conference on Church and Society. Official Report. Geneva: W.C.C., 1967.

The World Council of Churches. Minutes and Reports of the Meetings of the Central Committee.
The Tenth Meeting, Yale Divinity School, U.S.A., 1957.
The Eleventh Meeting, Nyborg Strand, Denmark, 1958.

The Twelfth Meeting, Rhodes, Greece, 1959.
The Seventeenth Meeting, Rochester, New York, U.S.A., 1963.
The Eighteenth Meeting, Enugu, Nigeria, 1965.
The Twenty-Third Meeting, Canterbury, Great Britain, 1969.

<u>World Development: The Challenge to the Churches</u>. Official Report of the Conference on World Co-operation for Development, Beirut, 1968. Geneva: Exploratory Committee on Society Development and Peace, 1968.

II. Unpublished Sources

Kitagawa, D.   "The World Council of Churches and the Race Problem: An Abstract." Geneva: File of the Secretariat on Racial and Ethnic Relations, undated. (Mimeographed.)

Strassberger, Elfriede. "Ecumenism in South Africa 1936 - 1960 with Special Reference to the Mission of the Church." Unpublished ThD thesis, University of Stellenbosch, 1971.

"Summary of Judgement in the Supreme Court of South Africa." Johannesburg: the Christian Institute, 1967. (Mimeographed.)

Visser't Hooft, W.A.   "Reflections on World Council of Churches' Action Concerning Interracial Relations." Address to the Notting Hill Consultation. Paper number 6/E. 1969. (Mimeographed.)

World Council of Churches Communication. "Blake, the Rev. Dr. Eugene Carson." Geneva: 1971. (Mimeographed.)

III. Published Books

Abrecht, P.   <u>The Churches and Rapid Social Change</u>, London: S.C.M., 1961.

Adler, Elisabeth.   <u>A Small Beginning</u>. Geneva: W.C.C., 1974.

Bennett, J.C. (ed.)   <u>Christian Social Ethics in a Changing World</u>. New York: Association Press, London: S.C.M., 1966.

Cawood, Lesley.   <u>The Churches and Race Relations</u>. Johannesburg: South African Institute of Race Relations, 1964.

De Vries, E. (ed.)   <u>Man in Community</u>. New York: Association Press, London: S.C.M., 1966.

Dickinson, R.   <u>Line and Plummet: The Churches and Development</u>. Geneva: W.C.C., 1968.

Ecumenical Statements on Race Relations: Development of Ecumenical Thought on Race Relations 1937 - 1964. Geneva: W.C.C., 1965.

Fey, H.E. (ed.) The Ecumenical Advance: A History of the Ecumenical Movement, Volume 2. London: S.P.C.K., 1970.

Goodall, N. Ecumenical Progress: a Decade of Change in the Ecumenical Movement 1961 - 71. London: O.U.P., 1972.

Grubb, Sir Kenneth G. Crypts of Power. London: Hodder and Stoughton, 1971.

Kitagawa, D. Race Relations and Christian Mission. New York: The Friendship Press, 1964.
The Pastor and the Race Issue. New York: The Seabury Press, 1965.

Lehmann, P. Ethics in a Christian Context. London: S.C.M., 1963.

Lloyd, R. The Church of England 1900 - 1965. London: S.C.M., 1966.

Oldham, J.H. Christianity and the Race Problem. London: S.C.M., 1924.

Pope, L. The Kingdom Beyond Caste. New York: The Friendship Press, 1957.

Populorum Progresio. Encyclical Letter of Pope Paul VI. London: Catholic Truth Society, 1967.

Preston, R.H. (ed.) Technology and Social Justice. London: S.C.M., 1971.

Ramsey, P. Who Speaks for the Church? Edinburgh: The St. Andrew Press, 1969.

Van den Heuvel, A.H. (ed.) Unity of Mankind: Speeches from the Fourth Assembly of the World Council of Churches, Uppsala 1968, Geneva: W.C.C., 1969.

Van der Bent, A.J. The Utopia of World Community: an Interpretation of the World Council of Churches for Outsiders. London: S.C.M., 1973

Vincent, J.J. The Race Race. London: S.C.M., 1970.

Visser't Hooft, W.A. Christianity, Race and South African People. Report: An Ecumenical Visit by the General Secretary of the World Council of Churches. New York: National Council of the Churches of Christ in the U.S.A., 1952.
Memoirs. London: S.C.M., 1973.
The Ecumenical Movement and the Race Problem. For the series "The Race Question and Modern Thought". Paris: UNESCO, 1954.

IV. Articles and Periodicals

Baldwin J. and   "White Racism or World Community?" The Ecumen-
Caradon, Lord   ical Review, XX, 4 (1968).

Crane, W.H.   "From the Politics of Consultation to those of
                  Confrontation," Study Encounter, 5 (1969).

Etheredge, D.A.   "Changing Prevailing Racial Patterns through
                  Economic Action," Race Relations in Ecumenical
                  Perspective, 5 (1964).

"Ethnic Tensions in an Emerging Nation - the Case of Ceylon", Race Relations in Ecumenical Perspective, 3 (1962).

Kitagawa, D.   "All in Each Place: Racial and Cultural Issues,"
                  The Ecumenical Review, XV, 1 (1962).

                  "Theological and Non-Theological Factors in Race
                  Relations," The Ecumenical Review, XIII, 3 (1961).

Matthews, Z.K.   "The Road from Non-Violence to Violence," Race
                  Relations in Ecumenical Perspective, 5 (1964).

"Statement of the Zagorsk Consultation," Study Encounter, 4 (1968).

Wendland, H.D.   "The Relevance of Eschatology for Social Ethics,"
                  The Ecumenical Review, V, (1953).

V. Other Sources

Correspondence from the Rev. Dr. Paul Abrecht, 12th March, 1974.

Correspondence from the Rev. David Gill, 17th October, 1973.

Personal Interview with the Rev. Dr. Norman Goodall, ex-Secretary of the I.M.C. and ex-Assistant General Secretary of the W.C.C., 1st April 1974.

St. Mark's Library
The General Theological Seminary
175 Ninth Avenue
New York, N. Y. 10011